THE 5 DECLASSIFIED ESTATE PLANNING SECRETS YOU CAN'T AFFORD TO IGNORE

WHAT YOU DON'T KNOW CAN SINK YOU AND YOUR FAMILY, CREATE UNNECESSARY STRESS AND FRUSTRATION, COST THOUSANDS OF DOLLARS, AND RESULT IN A FAMILY MELTDOWN

Linda M. Sherfey, Esq., USN RET

DEDICATION

This book is dedicated to God, my family, my husband Sol, my daughter Joanna, and my parents Roscoe and Mary Geyer.

Thank you to God who guides and sustains me.

Thank you to my husband, who inspires me to reach for the stars and is always supportive no matter how crazy my ideas are.

Thank you to my daughter for loving me and forgiving my shortcomings.

Thank you to my parents for always encouraging me to be great in all I choose to do, and who taught me the value of serving others and to live with integrity and seek excellence.

What Linda Sherfey's Clients Say You Will Like About Her

"I was afraid of high lawyer fees, concerned about sharing my personal information, and worried about my being indecisive. What I liked best about working with Linda is I got the best customer service. I like paying by the job and not by the hour. Linda is, for me, a down home professional. The main benefit I received was accomplishing a short-term goal that had been avoided <u>too</u> long and knowing that she is just a phone call away."
– **Nancy Marslender, Portsmouth, VA**

"By sharing her credentials and philosophy up front, Linda allows her clients to determine if this relationship will be compatible and sets the stage for a positive experience. To Linda, clients represent more than just a means to an income. She really enjoys her chosen area of her profession. Client satisfaction and peace of mind are her top priorities, because she sees her clients as a lifelong relationship. She is ethical, honest, and up front with her fees and doesn't pressure clients to purchase unneeded services. We had no idea what all was involved in setting up a trust, but she walked us through it with down to earth advice. Linda provides a valuable service that <u>everyone</u> needs, whether they know it or not!"
– **John and Gwen Vogt, Portsmouth, VA**

"Our biggest concerns before meeting Linda were trust, cost, and honesty. Linda impressed us with her honesty, quickly put us at ease, and answered all of our questions. She guided and helped us create our living trust, which leaves us feeling like the world has been lifted from our shoulders. Now we have peace of mind knowing that we have a complete financial estate plan

that assures us our wishes are met for our future medical and financial needs."
– Bill and Irma Smith, Norfolk, VA

"I was worried about the mess I would leave if I died without a will and if I would be happy with the final product. Linda was friendly and did a thorough job. I especially like her personal approach and didn't get the feeling that she is all about money."
– Dr. William "Si" Simonson, Suffolk, VA

"Other attorneys I previously worked with had their own agenda as to how I should set up my estate and did not do as well at listening to my wishes as Linda did. I really like her thoroughness and professionalism. Her friendly personality makes doing the tasks involved easier. Now I have the knowledge and confidence that my wishes will be carried out after my death."
– Sandy C., Chesapeake, VA

"We were impressed with Linda's entire approach to operating her business. She is not just a professional, but one who obviously enjoys her chosen work. Her up-front presentation of her qualifications and how she conducts her business put our minds at ease and gave us the confidence to choose her as the lawyer we wanted for a long-term relationship. Thanks to her practical advice in the development of our trust, we are very pleased with the thoroughness of our documents and comfortably feel we now have our affairs in order for our children to handle. Linda is ethical, honest, and has a dedicated relationship with her clients. She is not only an expert in estate planning and eldercare matters, but also thoroughly enjoys her work and spent the time necessary to ensure we understand the purpose and workings of our documents."
– Dick and Lorraine, Chesapeake, VA

"Linda did everything I wanted, and I feel sure that if I need her, she will be there for me. Linda listens to you and then helps you put together

what you want and need so that what you want to happen is what will happen. She explains everything in plain English. I am glad Linda helped me get my affairs in order in case something should happen to me."
– JC, Chesapeake, VA

"Linda has a friendly put you at ease attitude and treats you like family. She took lots of time, not just with me, but with me and my daughters. She never once made us feel rushed, but when appropriate, spoke only with me, ensuring complete confidentiality. Linda spoke in layman's terms with me, offered all the estate planning alternatives, and guided me to choose what I felt was best for me. The whole experience was very pleasant. I now have peace of mind."
– MVB, Portsmouth, VA

"I really enjoyed Linda's commitment to everything she discussed. She is very passionate about estate planning, which is very important to me and I would think to all others. Linda is very thorough and knowledgeable. The main benefit I received is self satisfaction. I know that all my stuff is in order now. I have peace of mind for my daughters when I pass."
– Mike Buck, Portsmouth, VA

"I was concerned about being a widow with no children. I didn't know how best to divide my assets. I wanted to be organized so that my siblings were not burdened if illness left me unable to handle my affairs. I really liked that Linda came to my home. She personally cares, and her approach was more effective than just business."
– M.E. Grubb, Suffolk, VA

"We heard Linda speak at a workshop. We felt she was very knowledgeable and we could trust her. We felt comfortable talking to Linda about our family situation, and she was able to accomplish what we needed. Linda is very thorough, and we were impressed with

her detail work. Linda is detail oriented and very easy to talk to."
– **A. & R. C., Suffolk, VA**

"Linda explained the whole process of what happens when you do not have a plan in place and how to fix that. She answered all my questions, no matter how silly they seemed. I now feel that my affairs are in order. It's a huge weight off my shoulders and off my mind! Linda made the process easy, explained everything, and handled everything in a warm, caring, but professional, manner."
– **Kathi V., Chesapeake, VA**

"Linda is very personable. Learning about estate planning was most pleasant. She made it easy to get my thoughts on paper. You'll love working with Linda!"
– **J.H., Portsmouth, VA**

WARNINGS!

— Think of this book as a primer. The book is not intended to answer all your questions, because your situation is unique. This book is intended to provide a foundation so you will have a good idea of what is possible when you come in for your appointment.

— Reading this book doesn't make us your estate planning attorney.

— Some of the information is specific to Virginia. Other states may have different rules.

— Names have been changed to protect confidentiality.

Special Offer from
Linda M. Sherfey, P.C.
The Estate Planning Solution

We don't want any barriers to stand in the way of you finding out about the

5 Declassified Estate Planning Secrets You Can't Afford to Ignore.

This book is designed to inform you before you meet with us.

After we meet, this book will be a reference to remind you of our discussions.

But wait, there's more!

You can meet with us for ninety minutes for a FREE estate planning consultation. This book is a general guide. During our meeting, we dive deep into your unique situation. You know your family, situation, and goals. We know the law. Together, we create a customized plan for you.

But wait, there's more!

When you bring this book with you to your FREE estate planning consultation, you will receive a $100 discount when choosing a complete estate plan.

You have this guide book—now you need your customized plan.

The waiting time to meet with us is two to four weeks. So call now, because you'll have plenty of time to finish reading this book before we meet.

Call 757-966-9700 right now to get started.

TABLE OF CONTENTS

INTRODUCTION

<u>You may be wondering about the book and chapter titles.</u>

What's with all the talk about a mission and having a battlegroup? I had a twenty-year career as an officer in the US Navy. I realize that estate planning is not a hot topic page-turner. I know you don't want to read a boring book about a law topic with unfamiliar words and descriptions. Therefore, I have used my navy background as a framework to assist you in discovering the five estate planning secrets.

In my own life's journey, I was completely clueless about estate planning until I was in law school. It saddens and scares me that you don't know what I know. So my mission is to write and speak about estate planning in a way that is not only informative, but also interesting. I've also provided a guide to help you chose your estate planning attorney in Appendix A.

So let's get you started, with my promise that you won't be bored and you will know the five estate planning secrets when you have finished reading this book.

<u>When submarines are submerged, you can't see them.</u>

You don't even know they are there. Issues in estate planning can be submerged and hidden out of your sight. You don't even know you may be putting your family in jeopardy of sinking when they are most vulnerable—after you are gone.

What if I told you:

- That thinking aging, illness, and incapacity are scary and talking about them seems unnecessary and too far away when we are well is dead wrong.

- Both accident and illness are unpredictable, no matter how good you feel.

So this book is for you if:

- You want to know what you don't know about estate planning.

- You have resisted or procrastinated because you don't know what to do and are afraid to ask.

- You want a better understanding of estate planning so you can more confidently answer questions when preparing an estate plan.

- You want a better understanding of the estate plan you already have and want to see if your attorney missed an important issue.

Why it's Essential for You to Get Your Estate Plan Shipshape Right Now

The navy keeps its ships and crew prepared and maintained all the time. The navy can't wait for an emergency to get the ships and crew built, trained, provisioned, and ready to get underway.

Unfortunately, both illness and accidents are unpredictable, no matter how good you feel.

I can't tell you how many times folks call for an appointment because they are scheduled for surgery. Aren't there enough things to do when scheduled for surgery besides see an attorney?

Hospitalization due to illness can also cause a crisis. Our office received a panicky call from Sam, who lives in Maine. Sam's mother, Becky, was seriously ill and in the intensive care unit of the hospital. Becky was the one who paid the bills and kept track of the finances for herself and her husband. Sam's dad, George, was frail from his ongoing battle with cancer. George needed a General Power of Attorney so his family could help him in his time of need. Fortunately, George was able to sign a General Power of Attorney so his children could help him. The sad fact is that his children had some sleepless nights until we could get George's General Power of Attorney signed.

An accident can change everything in an instant. Dorothy was doing fine in her mid-sixties. She was teaching part time and enjoying life. Her children told me that she was in her car following a pickup truck when a dresser fell off the truck and crashed into the windshield of her car. Dorothy's life changed in an instant. Although she did well recovering physically, Dorothy now has diminished mental capacity. It was too late for Dorothy to sign a General Power of Attorney. We had to go to court. Instead of Dorothy's children focusing on her, they were in a courtroom.

Cliff was ready to retire. His business was for sale, and he had a buyer. Cliff and his wife, Susan, had a motor home, and their plan was to hit the road when he retired. One day, Susan wasn't feeling well. She fainted. Susan was standing on their ceramic tile floor in the kitchen when she fainted. When you faint, you don't catch yourself, so she hit her head pretty hard. Her brain damage from the fall is permanent. Susan's symptoms resemble dementia. She cannot be left alone for a minute. Both their lives changed in an instant. Susan did not have a General Power of Attorney. Now Susan can't sign a General Power of Attorney, because she does not have the required mental capacity. It's too late.

I also hear over and over again that a loved one's death was completely unexpected and not following a long illness. My mother had a heart attack and was gone in a few hours. Until that day, she was fine and doing everything she wanted to. The truth is that we just don't know when we will die or possibly become mentally incapacitated. I had a client laugh at himself when he said "if I die." He quickly corrected himself and said "when I die."

You are reading the right book.

The answers are here.

Read on. Full throttle ahead.

Getting Started Guide: How to Best Use This Book to Guide You on Your Estate Planning Mission

Chapter 1 provides my background. The first section describes why I chose the field of estate planning and what my qualifications are. It is a short section, so please read it before continuing on. If you are curious, Appendix B lists all of my navy duty stations and responsibilities in detail.

Chapter 2 is a must read, because it provides an overview of all the documents you need in order to have a complete estate plan. Most folks just think about a will, but there is so much more. A will provides no benefits while you are alive. There are four estate planning documents designed to benefit you while you are alive.

Chapter 3 is a must read when you are ready to find an estate planning attorney. Not all attorneys are created equal. If you want a checklist of questions to ask when seeking an attorney, see Appendix A.

Chapter 4 is a must read only if you are thinking about doing it yourself with no guidance. This chapter describes what can happen if you sail away from the pier into open water with no charts, no compass, and no guidance system onboard.

Chapter 5 is a must read for a complete understanding of the basics of living trusts and wills. You'll find this chapter is an easy read in plain English.

Chapter 6 is a must read to find out about the four estate planning documents that benefit you while you are alive. One of these documents can save thousands of dollars in attorney fees if you have it.

Chapters 7–13 will be a must read depending on your situation. So feel free to pick and choose or skip altogether.

Chapter 7 is what is essential for seniors. If you are not a senior but have parents who are seniors, you should read this chapter for them or show it to them. You must read Chapters 5 and 6 to understand this chapter.

Chapter 8 is for parents who have adult children with problems such as an unstable marriage, poor money management resulting in debts, or alcohol or drug issues. Leaving an inheritance to them outright could cause a disaster and cause more harm than good.

Chapter 9 is for couples who have children from a previous relationship. There are so many things that can go wrong that this is a precarious situation for the surviving spouse and the deceased spouse's children.

Chapter 10 is for parents with minor children. This chapter discusses asset management for children, as well as naming a potential guardian to raise your children. If you are a grandparent, read this chapter and then show it to your kids with minor children.

Chapter 11 is for parents of special needs children AND husbands and wives that have mentally incapacitated spouses. A must read also if you have a parent with a mental incapacity.

Chapter 12 is for parents of pets. Read it if you care about what happens to your pet if you become mentally incapacitated, in addition to what happens to your pet when you die.

Chapter 13 is for unmarried partners. If this is not you, you can skip this chapter.

Chapter 14 explains why estate planning is not a one and done event. A must read if your estate planning documents are more than three years old.

Chapter 15 provides a step-by-step action plan for you. What you need to do next. A must read for everyone. There is an offer in this chapter that you are going to want to grab.

Declassified Secret #1:

Don't just retrieve your anchor and cast off, because there points you need to consider before getting underway and creating your estate plan.

Chapter 1: Why Listen to a Former Navy Officer About Estate Planning?

Chapter 1 provides my background. The first section describes why I chose the field of estate planning and what my qualifications are. It is a short section, so please read it before continuing on. If you are curious, Appendix B lists all of my navy duty stations and responsibilities in detail.

Chapter 2: What Kinds of Ships Do You Need in Your Estate Planning Battlegroup?

Chapter 2 is a must read because it provides an overview of all the documents you need in order to have a complete estate plan. Most folks just think about a will, but there is so much more. A will provides no benefits while you are alive. There are four estate planning documents designed to benefit you while you are alive.

Chapter 3: How to Choose a Powerful Commanding Officer/Attorney

<u>Chapter 3</u> is a must read when you are ready to find an estate planning attorney. Not all attorneys are created equal. If you want a checklist of questions to ask when seeking an attorney, see Appendix A.

CHAPTER 1

Why Listen to a Former Navy Officer About Estate Planning?

I was a jack-of-all trades with no specialty. Almost every new duty station brought new responsibilities and a new job to learn. Sometimes I would attend a navy school for job training, and sometimes I learned on the job. So I became very good at learning quickly. However, when you have only two to three years of experience, no one considers you to be an expert, and rightly so. I wanted my law career to be different and have a focus. Hmm, what to choose?

Why I Chose Estate Planning

While I was serving in the navy, my dad was diagnosed with Parkinson's disease. I happened to be home on leave and was with my parents at the doctor's office when they received the news. At that time, I didn't know anything about estate planning and long-term care planning, so I couldn't help my parents. Mom said Dad worried that the cost of his medicine— over $500 per month for just one of his prescriptions—would leave her with nothing. He had nightmares about it. I decided while in law school that my mission would be to help people like my parents, who found themselves without a plan and in a difficult position. I want my clients to have peace of mind.

So my practice has been and continues to be exclusively estate planning. For two years, I learned the basics at a law firm, doing only estate planning and learning about long-term care planning. Then I opened my own firm. I believe it is God's plan for me.

How My Law Firm is Different from Other Law Firms

One of the many aspects I like about estate planning is that it is possible to have a relationship with my clients. Unfortunately, the traditional estate planning experience is to meet with an attorney, sign your documents, get your documents, and then never hear from your attorney again. Estate planning doesn't have to be like this, with a complete disconnect at the end. As a matter of fact, the typical disconnect between an estate planning attorney and client is a huge mistake, because estate planning is not a one and done experience.

People's lives change, families change, and sometimes the law changes. People come to us to make changes to their documents. They tell us they can't find the attorney who drafted their documents. We don't want our clients to ever wonder where we are and how to get in touch with us. So when I started my own law firm, I added periodic estate plan review consultations to every estate plan as part of the package. By maintaining a relationship with our clients, they are encouraged to communicate with us when they have questions or want to make changes. To communicate with our clients, we publish a monthly newsletter to stay in touch. Our newsletter includes timely updates on estate planning issues, a yummy recipe, a personal note about what we've been up to and what is going on with our families, and more.

I also mail my newsletter to folks who are thinking about estate planning and want to get to know us better. If you are a Hampton Roads resident, you can get your own newsletter subscription for free by calling 757-966-9700 and just asking for it.

Another way we are different is every estate plan is personalized and customized, not standardized, so your estate plan is just right for you. We have lots of people tell us their situation is very simple—just leave everything to the children. However, when we start asking questions like "What do you want to happen to a child's share if they die before you do and that child has minor children?" clients quickly see they have not thought of everything. And why should they think of everything? It is not their job to think of everything—it's our job. We have seen lots of different scenarios, but we haven't seen them all. Because everyone is unique, we will never get tired of helping people with their estate plan. Your family is different is really true.

My Four-Step Estate Planning Solution Process

I have a four-step estate planning solution process for clients. The first step is a <u>Discovery Consultation</u>. We meet for as long as it takes so you can get to know us and we can get to know you and your situation. We only schedule two of these a day, so you won't ever feel rushed, and we won't be watching the clock. You will never have to wait in our reception room to see us. If you already have estate planning documents, we will provide a review of the documents you have and go over them with you. At the end of this consultation, we will determine the best estate plan for you together. At that time, we will quote a flat fee for your estate plan. No surprises and no meter running. During the process and after it is complete, you can always ask questions about your estate plan at no additional charge. You won't experience any pressure, and there is no obligation. We only want clients who like and trust us. We place a high value on our relationship.

When you decide to get underway on your estate plan, the next step in the process is the <u>Design Session</u>. The Design Session can begin immediately after the Discovery Consultation if you are ready and willing to get started. During the Design Session, we ask lots of questions so we know how to draft your documents so they will be just right for you. Don't worry if you don't have all the answers. We can work together to create the solution that is a perfect fit for you. If what you have in mind has serious pitfalls and is unlikely to turn out like you want, we'll discuss that too and devise a solution that will work to meet your goals.

The third step in the process is the <u>Document Review & Signing Session</u>. This session will be a couple of weeks after the Design Session. Together, we review the most important sections of your documents. Then the witnesses arrive and everyone signs. If you are signing living trust documents, we will also discuss your homework assignment, which is to fund your trust. Don't worry about understanding what we mean by funding your trust, as this step is described in Chapter 5, plus we provide unlimited guidance and will answer every funding question you have.

The fourth step in the process is the <u>Document Delivery Session</u>. This session will be a couple of weeks after the Document Review & Signing Session. We'll show you how your original documents are organized in your three-ring binder. We'll also talk about what you need to do next now that you have your original documents, such as safekeeping your original documents and which documents you need to make copies of for family and healthcare professionals. Don't worry about remembering everything we discuss about what you need to do next, because we give you a checklist that has step-by-step directions. We also send a letter to the people you have chosen to help you, such as your agents under a power of attorney and your personal representative (executor) for your will. These guidance letters to the people you have selected to provide a service to you accomplishes two things: (1) provide guidance on their duties and responsibilities; and (2) lets them know how to contact us if they have questions in the future. You receive a copy of these letters so you know the information they contain.

For a Review of My Navy Career, See Appendix B.

Chapter 2

What Kinds of Ships Do You Need in Your Estate Planning Battlegroup?

A battlegroup is a collection of military ships that travel together to accomplish a mission. Each ship in the battlegroup has a specific job to do that is different from the other ships in the battlegroup. For example, the aircraft carrier's job is surveillance from the air, air defense, and attack from the air. Not all battlegroups are composed of the same kinds of ships. The ships selected for the battlegroup is based on the battlegroup's mission.

Your first mission is the orderly distribution of your assets at your death.

It is understandable that most folks are concerned with what happens to their assets when they are gone. We all know that death is inevitable, so some people want to plan for it. The primary goal of planners is often to make the transition as easy as possible for their loved ones.

The ships essential for this mission are:

(1) an aircraft carrier – establishing and funding a living trust, or

(2) a supply ship – executing a Last Will & Testament.

The ships for distribution of assets at death are described in detail in Chapter Five. But there is another equally important mission.

The second mission is managing assets and providing decision-making capability in case you become mental disabled.

The disability planning mission provides benefits for you only while you are alive. The first component of the disability planning mission is planning for asset management while you are alive but unable to manage your assets yourself. The second component of the disability planning mission is healthcare management while you are alive but unable to manage your healthcare yourself.

We take for granted that people now live longer lives than in the past. The law has kept up to date with our increased longevity and improved medical techniques for keeping us alive longer. Although laws were passed to allow for disability planning, few people know about this mission planning opportunity and take advantage of it.

The ships essential for this mission are:

(1) a battleship – General Power of Attorney,

(2) a medical ship – a Healthcare Power of Attorney,

(3) a minesweeper – a Living Will, and

(4) a communications ship – an Authorization for Release of Protected Health Information.

The disability planning mission ships are described in detail in Chapter Six.

CHAPTER 3

What You Need to Look For in a Powerful Commanding Officer/Attorney

Is the attorney nice? Are they pleasant to talk to? Do they appear to be genuinely interested in you? Or does the attorney do all the talking and just wants to show you how smart they are?

Is the attorney a good listener?

An excellent attorney will ask you why you want an estate plan and then really listen to your answer. The best place to start is with your concerns and goals. The attorney should ask you a lot of questions about your family and your assets.

I was talking with a prospective client and reviewing her information and asset inventory. We talked about each of the children she had listed. She said she actually had one more child that she had not spoken to in many years. Kind of need to know that, because we need to address in her will that this child was not omitted in error. By not addressing the issue of the omitted child, the child could contest her will.

Is estate planning at least 75 percent of the attorney's practice?

Unfortunately, some attorneys think preparing a will once in a while is an easy way to add some extra income. Those attorneys don't help clients with probate, so they never see the possible problems that can arise with poorly drafted documents. For you to safely rely on the attorney's advice, you need to ask how many estate planning clients they prepare documents for in a year. There are form books available to attorneys. If that is what the attorney is relying on, the will form may not be the best plan for you. Additionally, what I see is that attorneys not well versed in estate planning don't discuss the other documents essential to a complete estate plan, such as a General Power of Attorney. So you get your will and think you are done, when in reality you are missing some vital estate planning documents.

I saw a will prepared by a real estate attorney and it was not pretty. Sam and Julie came to me to review and update their wills. At their real estate closing, the attorney offered to prepare wills for them. Real estate was the attorney's focus and where his experience was. Their wills had several flaws. The real estate attorney also didn't talk to Sam and Julie about the additional documents they needed for a complete estate plan. Fortunately, Sam and Julie came to see me, and I prepared a complete estate plan for them. Now not only do Sam and Julie have all their bases covered, they also have a relationship with me. They can call anytime and get their estate planning questions about their documents answered with no additional fee.

Did the attorney ask about your assets, like what bank do you use, what types of assets do you have, are the assets joint with someone else, have beneficiaries been named and if so, who are they?

Think about what happens when you meet with a doctor. The doctor's diagnosis is only as good as the information about your health that you provide. If you hold anything back, a misdiagnosis could happen, with bad results. The same holds true for attorneys. Your attorney needs to know everything about your assets. Confidentiality applies, and your attorney cannot share any information you provide without your consent.

Did the attorney describe the possible solutions, documents, and your estate plan in plain English?

Are they eager and happy to answer all your questions about their plan and their documents? You should never agree to an estate plan you don't understand. Diagrams can be very helpful. I create notes so my clients will be able to remember more of what we talk about. I prepare a trust diagram so clients can use the diagram to describe to children how their trust is designed to work instead of handing the sixty-page trust document to their children. I prepare an asset spreadsheet so clients with a trust will have a checklist for funding their trust or making the trust the beneficiary on an asset. When clients receive their documents at the Document Delivery Meeting, there is a lot to remember, so I give them a to-do checklist so they won't forget to do anything we talk about.

Did the attorney discuss the estate plan documents that benefit you while you are alive?

A will doesn't benefit you while you are alive. A will transfers your assets when you are not alive. Estate planning documents that benefit you while you are alive are: General Power of Attorney, Healthcare Power of Attorney, Living Will, Release of Protected Health Information, and a living trust. A complete estate plan will also include the documents that will benefit you now.

I received a frantic phone call from Fred asking for a General Power of Attorney for his girlfriend. She had Stage 4 cancer, was in a coma, and not expected to live long. Sorry, but it was too late to do anything. She can't sign a document if she is unconscious. The hospital asked Fred if she had a General Power of Attorney. Without a General Power of Attorney, nobody was going to have access to her assets. Nobody could pay her bills or make any financial decisions for her. At that point, in order to pay her bills for her, Fred's only alternative was to go to court to be appointed as her conservator. Conservator appointment costs thousands of dollars and takes time. Probably more time than she had.

Does the attorney require at least one alternate agent on your power of attorneys, executor for your will, or successor trustees for your living trust?

You must have legal capacity to sign estate planning documents. If the person you named as your agent under a power of attorney, executor for a will, or successor trustee of a living trust, dies, cannot serve, or just doesn't want to serve, your document becomes worthless. You must have at least one alternate. I can't tell you how many times I've reviewed someone's documents and noticed that there is no alternate listed. The one thing I absolutely insist on is naming an alternate. Together, we determine who a suitable alternate would be.

Two grandchildren came to see me about their grandmother, Edna. Edna had a General Power of Attorney naming her only child Lisa as her agent. Lisa was paying her mother's bills and managing her assets—until Lisa died. Edna's General Power of Attorney did not list an alternate agent. Edna couldn't sign a new General Power of Attorney because she had dementia. The only alternative for the grandchildren was to ask the court to appointment them as their grandmother's conservator. The mistake of not naming an alternate on Edna's General Power of Attorney cost Edna thousands of dollars. In addition, her nursing home bill was not paid for several months while the process of appointing a conservator proceeded. Going to court for conservator appointment could have been avoided by simply having an alternate agent listed on Edna's General Power of Attorney.

If you are a senior, does the attorney have long-term care planning knowledge?

The rules for a General Power of Attorney are that if the power is not included in the document, then your agent doesn't have permission to use that power. There are certain long-term care planning powers that need to be included in a General Power of Attorney for seniors. I call them "senior super powers." An example of a senior super power is giving permission to a child who is acting as your agent to pay themselves for taking care of you. The standard rules for a General Power would not allow an agent to pay themselves for any service to you. But you can create an exception by including this senior super power. See <u>Chapter 7</u> for more information on this topic.

For a comprehensive list of the
Ten Questions You Must Ask Before Choosing an Estate Planning
Attorney, see Appendix A.

Declassified Secret #2

Estate planning is not a do-it-yourself project, because mistakes won't be discovered until it's too late.

Chapter 4: Why Going into Battle All Alone Can Spell Disaster and Torpedo Your Family

Chapter 4 is a must read only if you are thinking about doing it yourself with no guidance. This chapter describes what can happen if you sail away from the pier into open water with no charts, no compass, and no guidance system onboard.

CHAPTER 4

Why Going into Battle All Alone Can Spell Disaster and Torpedo Your Family

I confess that I tend to be a do it yourselfer. However, over the years I have learned my limits the hard way. With most things, if it doesn't work out, you can always hire a professional to fix it or just live with the imperfections. With estate planning, if it doesn't work out, you might not be able to fix it. Problems with your will won't be discovered until you are gone. Limitations caused by missing powers in a General Power of Attorney won't be correctable if you have become mentally incapacitated and can't legally sign a new, more complete General Power of Attorney.

When I started my law firm, I went to an attorney to help me incorporate my business. I didn't want to spend the time to research business incorporation. More importantly, I did not want to have the nagging worrisome thoughts in the back of my mind of did I do it right. If my law firm business was ever sued, it would be too late to fix it.

Proceed with caution when using the Internet, magazines, and newspapers for legal research.

Each state has its own interpretation of what the estate planning laws should be. Jack decided to research property deeds online. On a major insurance company's website, he found information about a type of deed called a transfer on death deed. Jack asked me about doing a transfer on death deed for him. At that time, I had to advise him that a transfer on death deed was not legal in Virginia. I also talked to Susan, who was trying to administer her father's estate. She looked up the statutes for Virginia online, but didn't know that case law also applied. Case law is researching trial cases to see how the law was applied by a judge.

Can you live with the worry of wondering if you did your estate plan right? Did you think of everything? The harsh reality is that when you are gone, or if you lose your mental capability, it's too late to fix any problems.

Documents obtained online or from purchased software have their own hidden hazards.

How do you know you have signed the document correctly? Ed told me that he was the administrator of his father's estate. His dad, Henry, thought he had a will to take care of his estate when he died. However, Henry ordered his will online. Evidently, Henry thought that the draft was what he was supposed to sign. Henry must have sat at his kitchen table to read it, and then he just signed it. A short time later, Henry died. Ed took his dad's will to the probate clerk. The clerk could not accept Henry's will because no witnesses had signed, and Henry's will was not notarized. If Henry had an estate planning attorney's help, his will would have been executed properly and been accepted by the probate clerk. Instead, Ed had to find out the hard way that his dad's estate was going to be messy and possibly expensive.

Here is another example of someone thinking they have a will, but in reality they don't. I have a client named Bill who had his will prepared by the military right before he left for Vietnam. He later discovered that his will did not contain a self-proving affidavit. The self-proving affidavit's purpose is to make it unnecessary for the witnesses to the signing to show up in person when the will is probated. Can you imagine trying to find someone you never knew? The military witnesses were long gone and may have died. If your will doesn't have a self-proving affidavit, and at least one witness can't be located, that will is useless. So for more than twenty years, Bill thought he had a valid will. What if Bill had not realized that there was a problem with his will? Bill's family would have had a rude awakening at his death. Do you really want to take a chance?

Read the fine print, and you will discover that the online estate planning programs warn you they might not work. Scary!

And if you do it yourself, who will your family turn to when they have a question or need help? I have another client named Sally who had a mental breakdown sometime after she signed her documents that I prepared. Sally does not have any children, so she named her friend, Betty, to make medical decisions for her. Betty called my office in a panic. She couldn't find her copy of the Healthcare Power of Attorney that Sally had signed naming Betty as the person Sally wanted to make medical decisions for her. If Sally had created her Healthcare Power of Attorney herself, Betty's situation would have been hopeless. Instead, I was able to e-mail Sally's Healthcare Power of Attorney to Betty. She had a copy of the Healthcare Power of Attorney in minutes. I was also able to provide legal guidance to Betty when using the power of attorney.

An experienced estate planning attorney knows the right questions to ask. Bob and Mary told me that they wanted their daughter-in-law, Amy, to receive their son's inheritance if their son died before they did. Bob and Mary said their son had been married a long time, and they loved Amy like a daughter. I asked a vital question: "Would you want Amy to receive your son's inheritance if they were already divorced when he died?" "No way," they said in surprise. In that case, we would need to put the condition in their will or trust that their son must still have been married to Amy when he died.

An experienced estate planning attorney can make suggestions to assist in the smooth and easy transition of assets at death. I represented Brenda, a second wife, in the administration of her husband Frank's estate. Frank had two children from his first marriage. Brenda's relationship with Frank's children seemed to be fine—until he died. The afternoon of Frank's funeral, his daughter came to Brenda's home and proceeded to list all her grievances against Brenda. Apparently, Brenda's relationship with Frank's children was not as good as they had thought.

Frank's will left everything to his children. However, without any assistance from an estate planning attorney, Frank wrote a codicil (amendment) to his will. The change Frank wanted was for his two children to receive a two-thirds share and for Brenda to receive one-third share of the proceeds from the sale of Frank's home. I pointed out to Brenda that because of the wording of the codicil, if she died, her one-third of the proceeds from the sale of the home would evaporate. I also told her that all Frank's children had to do was refuse to sell the home and wait until she died. As an experienced estate planning attorney, I would have proposed as a possible solution that Frank's will state his executor was directed to sell the home and divide the proceeds. An executor is under court supervision, and Brenda would have received her money.

An experienced estate planning attorney can advise you on whether or not to name beneficiaries on your assets. Joanne came to see me about her son Steven's inheritance. Joanne and Steven's dad were divorced. Steven's dad had a $100,000 life insurance policy that named Steven as his beneficiary. Steven was seventeen years old when his dad died. Joanne's question was how could she keep from giving the $100,000 to Steven when he had his eighteenth birthday? Steven was looking at expensive cars, and the $100,000 would be gone within a year. I had to tell Joanne that it was too late. She must give all $100,000 to Steven on his eighteenth birthday.

If Steven's dad had seen an experienced estate planning attorney, the $100,000 could have been managed by someone Steven's dad chose before turning it over to Steven when he was older and more experienced with money. The money manager would have been under court supervision, so Steven's inheritance would be protected. The money manager that Steven's dad chose would have been able to spend Steven's inheritance on him for whatever he needed. However, instead of the shiny red Corvette convertible Steven said he needed, the money manager could have made the wise financial decision to buy a more practical car with Steven's money, so he would have a car—just not the car of Steven's dreams. The money manager could have spent Steven's inheritance on college tuition, rent, medical, even a down payment on a house. The idea here is that the money manager Steven's dad picked would have experience with money and know how to spend it wisely. Then at the age that Steven's dad picked, such as twenty-four, the money manager would turn over any remaining inheritance money to Steven. The big problem with a child receiving their inheritance at age eighteen is that they just are not experienced with money.

Another issue is that the online or book estate planning forms have to be generic so they have a chance of success in every state. Generic means you won't be able to take advantage of estate planning tools that may be unique to your state. For example, in Virginia, you don't have to list specific items to be given to specific people in your will. In the past, if you wanted to leave your china set to your oldest daughter, you needed to list that gift in your will. If you changed your mind, you had to sign a new will. Now Virginia will let you state in your will that you might make a separate list of specific items to go to specific people. If you make such a list, it legally becomes part of your will when you die. Your executor has the responsibility of making sure that the items listed in your separate list are distributed to the people you named. In Virginia, you can update the list as many times as you want in your handwriting in the comfort of your home because it doesn't have to be witnessed or notarized. You won't find the ability to make a list like this online or in book forms because it isn't possible in every state.

There is no way you can know what is possible and what the consequences can be. Estate planning is just not that simple.

If you do it yourself, your family will not know who to turn to if they need help. We stay in touch with our clients so they and their family will know who to call. We keep copies of their documents. We are only a phone call away in a time of crisis or just to ask a question. Who will help and guide you in making the best decisions? Who will your family turn to if you create your documents online? Who will you turn to for advice? Who will you turn to for an answer to your questions?

Declassified Secret #3

It's a dangerous myth that a will is all you need: essential ship types you need to know aboutfor an unsinkable estate plan.

Chapter 5: Asset Transfer: Trusts and Wills: Knowing the Differences Between an Aircraft Carrier and a Supply Ship

Chapter 5 is a must read for a complete understanding of the basics of living trusts and wills. You'll find this chapter is an easy read in plain English.

Chapter 6: Disability: How to Prepare for the Possibility of Engine Damage

Chapter 6 is a must read to find out about the four estate planning documents that benefit you while you are alive. One of these documents can save thousands of dollars in attorney fees if you have it.

Chapter 5

Asset Transfer: Trusts and Wills: Knowing the Difference Between an Aircraft Carrier and a Supply Ship

A supply ship has one mission, which is to transfer and deliver supplies to ships at sea. A will transfers and delivers assets to your beneficiaries under the supervision of the court. A supply ship performs its mission very well, just like a will does. However, a supply ship is not versatile or flexible and has its limitations. A will is like a supply ship because it gets the job done. Asset transfer at death using a will is not as easy and versatile as a living trust.

The mission of the aircraft carrier is both offensive and defensive air support at any location reachable by sea. An aircraft carrier is also like a small city. An aircraft carrier will have housing, a cafeteria, a barber and beauty shop, small grocery and department store, gym, and bank. All these activities support the aircraft carrier, its crew, and the mission. A living trust will manage, transfer, and deliver assets to your beneficiaries with no court involvement. What makes a living trust even more powerful than a will is that a trust can manage your assets while you are alive, whereas (you didn't think I could write a book about legalities without at least one 'whereas' did you?) a Last Will & Testament is only effective at death.

The Aircraft Carrier: Living Trust

First, I'm going to describe why a living trust is the premiere asset management and transfer ship, how a living trust is created, important terms you need to know, how a living trust is funded, and how a living trust operates.

Reasons Why a Living Trust Is Better

<u>The most important advantage to having a living trust is that it makes it really *easy* for someone to manage your assets and pay your bills if you become mentally incapacitated, AND a living trust makes it really *easy* for your assets to be distributed or managed for a beneficiary after you are gone.</u>

If the current trustee becomes mentally incapacitated, the rules can state that the successor trustee then has the authority and responsibility to manage the trust assets for the beneficiaries. A well-written trust will define how to determine if the trustee has become incapacitated, such as two physicians must agree. The asset management transition from one trustee to another is easy.

A living trust makes it easy to transfer assets to your beneficiaries. When you have passed on, the successor trustee just reads the trust rules to see what they are to do with the trust assets. The successor trustee can sell or retitle any trust property. There is no court oversight in the management or distribution of trust assets. The successor trustee has the authority to just do it, completely privately and with no court intervention.

<u>The second advantage is that living trusts are very flexible, because a living trust can continue to manage assets long after you are gone.</u> For example, let's say that Frank and Joan are in a second marriage for both of them.

They are living in Frank's home, and Frank wants his home to ultimately go to his two children. At the same time, Frank wants for Joan to continue living in his home as long as she wants to. Hmmm…the easiest and most practical way to accomplish both of Frank's goals is to have his home owned and controlled by the living trust. The living trust rules can state that Joan can stay in the home as long as she wants, and when she is no longer in the home, ownership will transfer to Frank's children. See <u>Chapter 10</u> for more examples.

A living trust can also manage assets for minor children, disabled children, or a child with drug/alcohol or credit problems. Their trust assets can be completely protected from their creditors and protected in case of divorce.

<u>The third advantage of a living trust is its ability to own property in multiple states and thereby avoid probate in multiple states.</u> Since the trust is its own legal entity, it can own property in any state. A living trust makes out-of-state property management EASY at death. The successor trustee reviews the trust distribution rules and either sells the property or signs a deed to transfer ownership of the property from the trust to a beneficiary.

For example, Tim and Edna live in Virginia, so if they had a will it would be probated in Virginia, their state of residence. Tim and Edna also own a beach house in North Carolina. Their will would also have to go through the probate process in North Carolina to transfer that property to their children. Probate in some states can be long and expensive. However, I have good news. If Tim and Edna have a living trust, the trust can own and control both their Virginia property and the North Carolina property. This means there will be no probate in Virginia and even better, no additional probate in North Carolina to transfer the properties to their beneficiaries.

My parents had a living trust. Their Florida home was correctly titled to trust ownership. When both of them were gone, a problem became visible. The land they still owned in Indiana was not titled to trust ownership. This did not come to light until a buyer wanted to purchase the Indiana property. Because the land had to go through Indiana probate, the real estate closing took seven months. If the buyer had not been patient, the sale of the Indiana property would have been lost.

The fourth advantage to a living trust is privacy. All of the terms of a living trust are completely private. Trust asset management and distribution is private. When a will is submitted for probate, it is recorded in the public records. This is why you sometimes see what is in a famous person's will in the newspaper or online. But wait, there is more! In Virginia, an executor must initially submit an inventory of all estate assets the executor is responsible for and then annually submit an accounting listing estate assets and expenses. The inventory and annual accountings are recorded and become a public record available to anyone.

The fifth advantage to a living trust is trust assets are immediately available for a beneficiary's benefit. If parents die and have a minor child or a disabled child, the trust assets are immediately available to the successor trustee to use for the care of the child. If parents leave assets to a minor child or a disabled child in a will, the assets will not be immediately available, because the estate has to be managed by the court process. The court process can take months or even years.

The sixth advantage of a living trust is mobility. If the grantors move to a different state, they can move their trust with them. For example, the trust rules can state that the trust will be governed by the laws of the Commonwealth of Virginia. A simple amendment to the trust can state that now the trust "lives" in Florida and will be governed by the laws of Florida. The purpose in changing the rules to state that Florida law will govern the trust is to make it more convenient for the grantors and trustees to get legal advice from an attorney in Florida. The trust could just as easily "stay" in Virginia under Virginia law. In either case, ownership of trust assets would not have to be changed again. Once trust assets are titled to the trust, the grantors don't have to change title again. I have clients who moved to North Carolina. They decided not to move their trust to North Carolina, because they want me to continue to be their estate planning attorney and for me to continue to provide legal advice about their trust.

Laying the Keel for a Living Trust

The most common type of trust is the revocable living trust. Revocable simply means that the grantor (also called settlor or trustor) can change their mind, remove trust assets from the trust, and dissolve the trust.

To describe a revocable living trust, I'm going to depart from the navy comparisons and use a business comparison instead. When I started my law firm, I signed a document called Articles of Incorporation. By signing the Articles of Incorporation, I created a legal entity. The document that creates a living trust is called a Declaration of Trust, or Trust Agreement. When the grantor(s) sign the Declaration of Trust document, a legal entity is created. It is just that easy. This legal entity called a trust owns assets and has rules for the management of those trust assets.

There are three parties to a trust. The first is the <u>grantor</u>(s). There can be more than one grantor, as is usually the case for a married couple. They are both the grantors. The grantor(s) is the rule maker. Only the grantor(s) can change the trust rules. An example of a trust rule is naming who the beneficiaries are.

The second party is the <u>trustee</u>(s). There can be more than one trustee, as is usually the case for a married couple. The grantor(s) decides who the current trustee(s) will be and who the future successor trustees will be. The grantor(s) also decides what powers the trustee(s) will have in the management of trust assets. The trustee(s) is responsible for the management of trust assets.

The third party to the trust is the <u>beneficiary</u>(s). The trust assets are managed by the trustee for the benefit of the beneficiary(s). There are current beneficiaries, as in the case of parents and minor children. For parents with adult children, the current beneficiaries would normally be the parents only. In the Declaration of Trust, the grantor(s) would name who the future beneficiary(s) will be when all the current beneficiaries are gone. So in the case of two parents, the trust rules can state that as long as one of them is living, the trust assets are for the benefit of the survivor, and when both of them are gone, the remaining trust assets will be distributed to their children. Only the grantor(s) can change who the beneficiary(s) is.

<u>Step one is to create the trust by the grantor(s) signing the Declaration of Trust.</u> The Declaration of Trust can be lots of pages or just a few. I prefer long trusts, because a long trust can contain more guidance. If your Declaration of Trust contains all the rules for managing trust assets, then you know what the rules are. If your Declaration of Trust just contains a few rules or no rules for managing trust assets, then the state statutes concerning trusts will be the decision maker instead of your trust. I would rather you be able to read the trust rules in your trust document and know what they are. The state statutes are the default rules. The statutes only apply if your trustee has a question about trust management and your trust doesn't have an answer contained in your trust's rules. If the statutes don't provide an answer to a trustee question, the last alternative is to have a court judge provide a solution. A judge's solution is the most costly, slowest, and you won't be able to predict the outcome.

For example, say you have named your son Frank as the successor trustee, and you are the current trustee. You are showing signs of dementia. You are forgetting to pay bills, and the power was almost turned off at your home. You think you are fine. How will Frank know when he can legally take over the management of the trust assets as your successor trustee?

Remember that an advantage of a trust is that the successor trust can manage trust assets while you are alive but unable to manage assets yourself. In the Declaration of Trust we use, the rules provide a procedure for the successor trustee to follow if they need to take over the management of trust assets while the current trustee is alive. All Frank needs to do is read the Declaration of Trust to see what he must do. If the trust didn't provide an answer, Frank would have to look at the statutes. They are available online, but how convenient is that? If Frank has a question that is not answered in the Declaration of Trust document and isn't answered in the statutes, then Frank will have to seek guidance from a judge. Who knows what the answer will be in that case? Another advantage of having the rules spelled out in the trust is that you can have it your way instead of the statute's way. Remember that the state statutes are just the default rules.

Step two is to fund the trust. Now that the trust as a legal entity exists, the trust needs to have assets to control. A critical step in establishing a trust is transferring ownership of the grantor's assets to the trust. The trust becomes the legal title holder of the assets for the beneficiary.

For example, the name of the trust is the Dagwood and Blondie Bumstead Living Trust dated April 1, 2014. The name of the trust can be anything you want, but the name includes the date that the Declaration of Trust was signed. Assets such as an investment account, bank account, certificate of deposit, and car would be retitled with the name of the trustees followed by the name of the trust. For example, Dagwood T. Bumstead and Blondie C. Bumstead, Trustees of the Dagwood and Blondie Bumstead Living Trust dated April 1, 2014.

Is there work involved in the transfer of assets? Yes! Remember, I stated at the beginning that a trust makes it easy to distribute assets at your death. That is because you as the grantor have already done the work. With a will, you don't have to do any transfer of asset ownership because that is your executor's job. The work doesn't happen with a will until you are gone, and then your executor gets to do it.

To retitle assets to a trust means that the grantor must contact every entity holding assets, such as a bank holding a checking account, and fill out paperwork to transfer ownership of that asset to the trustee. The trust can also own real property such as your home, a second home in another state, and a deeded timeshare. A new deed is required to transfer the property to trust ownership. No transfer tax is due on the transfer deed because you are making a gift to your trust. This transfer also shouldn't trigger a due on sale requirement by your lender. In other words, a mortgage payoff won't be triggered by transferring your property to trust ownership.

The good news is this asset transfer of ownership only happens once. When you transfer ownership of a savings account at a bank to your trust, a new account and new checks are not required.

You wouldn't normally transfer ownership of life insurance or an IRA to a trust, but a trust can be the beneficiary of life insurance or an IRA.

To guide clients, my policy is to prepare an asset spreadsheet with specific instructions for each asset on whether the title is to change to the trust or if the trust is to be the beneficiary. The spreadsheet of your assets becomes your to-do list. This step is so important that we are available for unlimited questions and guidance with no additional fee.

I met with Lorraine, who had a do-it-yourself fill in the blanks trust. She has one son and several grandchildren. Lorraine listed her son as either joint owner on her assets or as the beneficiary. Her trust document showed that she wanted to leave different percentages of her assets to her grandchildren. None of her assets had been transferred to trust ownership. Lorraine had missed this important step. I advised her that because her trust did not own any assets and was empty, and her son's name was on all her assets or the beneficiary of everything she had except for her home, that her grand-children would receive nothing. Lorraine said, "I don't like what you are telling me." I replied that I was only telling her the truth.

A trust only controls assets it owns. Your management of trust assets as the current trustee is just like it is now. As the trustee, you have complete control to buy, sell, and gift trust assets. Remember that trust ownership of assets means your co-trustee or successor trustee can manage trust assets in case of your disability, in addition to your death. An additional benefit of a trust is that it is EASY for the successor trust to have access to assets and immediate control of those assets. With a living trust, there is no waiting time like there is for probating a will. For some estate plans, immediate access to assets is critical, as in the case of minor children or family members with special needs. See Declassified Secret #3: Rough Seas That Can Throw Your Estate Plan Off Course.

Reporting income on trust assets is easy. Having a trust won't make life more complicated. If the trust has assets that produce income, that income passes through to the grantor(s) and is reported on the grantor(s) tax return. When a person dies, their social security number also dies. So only when all grantors are gone, will a trust need its own tax identification number and need to file its own tax return to report trust income to the IRS.

Only the grantor(s) can change the trust rules. When managing trust assets, the trustees are required to follow the trust rules found in the Declaration of Trust. The grantor(s) can make minor adjustments to the trust with an amendment. If the trust needs an overhaul, the entire trust can be revised with a restatement. What doesn't change is the name of the trust. You don't want to change the name of the trust because then the trust assets would have to be retitled in the new name of the trust. When the grantor(s) is deceased, the rules can't be changed.

<u>Trustee accountability is to the beneficiary(s).</u> Since there is no court oversight of the trustee of a trust, it is up to the beneficiaries to stay aware of what the trustee is doing with trust assets. Watching trust assets is easy when the trustee is the same person as the beneficiary. Let's say the trustee is not a beneficiary. A trustee is accountable to the beneficiary. The trustee must keep records of all trust financial transactions. The trustee would provide accountings to the beneficiary as required by the trust rules.

<u>The Trustee is compensated.</u> The trust rules normally provide that the trustee can be paid for the responsibility of managing trust assets. The trustee is not required to pay themselves as trustee. The rate can be specified in the trust rules or the trust rules can state that the trustee will be paid the then standard rate. Currently, the standard rate is 1 1/2 percent based on the value of trust assets. Usually, the percentage goes down as the amount of trust assets goes up, on a graduated scale. For comparison, executors commonly receive 5 percent of the value of estate assets as compensation. Executors have a more difficult job in gathering the estate assets and reporting estate management accounting to the court.

<u>A regular revocable living trust does not provide asset protection</u>. A revocable living trust will not provide the grantors with creditor protection or asset protection when applying for government benefits such as Medicaid. Since the trust is revocable, the grantors can retitle trust assets to remove them from the trust and give trust assets back to the grantors free from the trust rules. For asset protection, a different type of trust is needed. For more information on asset protection, see <u>Chapter 7</u>.

<u>The trust continues on even after the grantor is deceased</u>. The trust outlives the grantor(s). When the grantor(s) dies, the rules can't be changed, but the trust does not immediately end. Because the trust is a legal entity, it continues on just like a business does when the owner dies. When I die, my law firm continues as a legal entity as long as it needs to. A trust can

continue on as long as it needs to. The successor trustee pays any outstanding bills and files a final tax return for the deceased's current beneficiary (i.e., parent). The successor trustee continues to manage trust assets for the benefit of the successor beneficiary(s) (i.e., children). The successor trustee reviews trust rules for the correct distribution of trust assets to the successor beneficiary and then follows those rules. For more information about how a trust can continue to hold assets for the beneficiary, see <u>Secret #3 Rough Seas That Can Throw Your Estate Plan Off Course.</u>

<u>There are many different types of living trusts.</u> A complete description of all the different types of living trusts is beyond the scope of this book. You should find a competent attorney using the guidelines of Chapter 4 to determine the best fit for you and your goals.

A Pour Over Will complements a living trust. The purpose of a Pour Over Will is to transfer any assets not already titled to the trust and not having any beneficiary, using the probate process. Think of the Pour Over Will as a safety net. Probate is not an ideal way to transfer assets to the trust. Probate assets must go through probate with court involvement. However, a will is the only way to have a voice after you are gone to name who would raise minor children as their guardian if something happens to you. A Pour Over Will would also have guardian of minor children provisions.

The Supply Ship: Last Will & Testament

A supply ship has one mission, which is to transfer and deliver supplies to ships at sea. A will transfers and delivers assets to your beneficiaries under the supervision of the court. A supply ship performs its mission very well, just like a will does. However, a supply ship is not versatile or flexible and has its limitations. A will is like a supply ship because it gets the job done.

Which assets does a will control?

A common misconception is that a will controls everything. That is not true! Here is critical information—a will only controls an asset in your name alone, with no beneficiary. This is a difficult concept for a lot of people to grasp. Everyone thinks their will shall control all their assets. Read this paragraph again.

An excellent example of this truth is a life insurance policy. You fill out a form telling the life insurance company who the beneficiary is. When you die, your beneficiary just has to complete a form for the life insurance company and return it along with a death certificate to receive the benefit check. Your will has no say over who receives the life insurance proceeds as long as there is a living beneficiary. It's a different story if your beneficiary dies before you do. If you haven't updated your life insurance policy with a new beneficiary, the life insurance company will not know who is to receive the policy benefit.

The question of who the life insurance company will pay the benefit to if your named beneficiary is deceased will be answered in one of three ways:

(1) if you don't have a will, your state will have a statute that says who will receive any asset with no beneficiary, and you will have no say in that decision. The statutes generally state your spouse first, then children, then grandchildren, then parents, and so on. Usually, the state statute will list a blood relative after your spouse. The state statutes make sense because the issue of what happens to an asset at death needs to be settled;

(2) even if you do have a will, some banks, insurance companies, and investment holders have their own rules about who the beneficiary will be; and

(3) if you do have a will, you don't have to accept the state's plan for distribution of your assets. YOU decide and you control who receives your assets at death.

When I explained to Ed how the statute works to transfer his assets at his death, Ed emphatically said that he did NOT want for his brother to get everything he had. To have it Ed's way, he needed to have his choice of beneficiary named on all of his assets and have a will as a backup.

Some asset ownership passes automatically

First, any asset owned jointly with the right of survivorship will automatically belong to the survivor at the death of the joint owner. If spouses own a home jointly with survivorship, when one dies, the home automatically belongs to the survivor. If you have a child named as a joint owner on your checking account so they can write checks for you, then the account will belong to that child automatically at your death. The child can share with siblings or not. It will be their choice.

Second, if you have a beneficiary, payable on death or transfer on death name on an asset, that asset will automatically belong to the person you named. The named person will just need to present a death certificate to have the asset transferred to their name.

Advantages of Having a Will

Benefits of having a will are:

(1) you choose who will receive your assets,

(2) you can decide when your heirs will receive their assets,

(3) you can decide who will manage your estate, and

(4) in Virginia, a will is the only way prospective guardians can be named for minor children.

Disadvantages of Using a Will

Disadvantages of using a will are:

(1) it is only effective at your death and does nothing to assist in asset management while you are alive,

(2) if you have real property (such as a second home) in a different state than the state you live in, there will be probate in your state of residence and an additional probate in the state where your property is located,

(3) it will usually take longer for heirs to receive their inheritance due to the probate process,

(4) a will is less flexible than a living trust in management of assets for heirs due to the limitations of court involvement,

(5) in some states probate is expensive, and

(6) all your financial information is made public because the inventory and accountings are recorded.

Sometimes people focus on what will happen to their assets at death, but forget about asset management while they are alive yet not able to manage their assets themselves.

Sam told me he named his spouse Betty as his beneficiary on their IRA. That's great, but Betty will not be able to access that asset to pay for Sam's care before his death if Sam became mentally incapacitated. Betty only gets control *after* Sam's death. To manage Sam's IRA while he is still alive but not able to do it himself, Betty will need a General Power of Attorney. <u>See Chapter 6: Disability: How To Prepare For The Possibility of Engine Damage.</u>

A Trust That Is Created By a Will

<u>A testamentary trust is created by a will after you are gone.</u> A living trust is created while you are alive. The will can contain a trigger that activates a testamentary trust if conditions stated in the will exist at the time of death.

For example, a will can protect assets for younger beneficiaries by establishing a testamentary trust. A will can say that IF a beneficiary is under the age that you pick—let's say twenty-four—their inheritance will not be given to them outright, but instead held in a testamentary trust. If when you die there are no beneficiaries under the age of twenty-four, the testamentary trust is not needed and the beneficiaries receive their inheritance outright. If a beneficiary is under the age of twenty-four when you die, their inheritance is held for their benefit in trust. It is possible for the testamentary trust assets to pay for tuition, rent, food, medical, clothes, a car, down payment on a home, or even a wedding.

Your will would state the rules for the testamentary trust and who would manage the trust assets. The person you pick to manage the trust assets is called the trustee. The trustee would need to qualify with the probate clerk to receive the beneficiary's assets from the executor. The trustee is bonded with surety and responsible for annual accountings to show what they are doing with the assets. Bonding with surety means that if the trustee misuses the assets under their control, the bond company will refund the money to the trust. Then the bond company seeks repayment from the trustee. This way, trust assets are totally protected. There is a charge for the bond, which would be paid from trust assets. Your choice of trustee must be someone with good credit, because they have to qualify for the bond. The court maintains oversight of the testamentary trust's assets by requiring the trustee to provide annual accountings with bank account statements, investment statements, and receipts for expenses.

Advantages to a Testamentary Trust

One advantage to a trust created by a will is that a testamentary trust's assets are protected, the court has oversight, and the trustee can spend the trust assets on the beneficiary. The reason for this type of testamentary trust is that the trustee will have better judgment than the beneficiary. The beneficiary may be too young to handle an inheritance, may be mentally incapacitated and can't manage money, may have difficulty managing money and have creditor problems, or may have drug, gambling, or alcohol issues.

Another advantage is that the testamentary trust's assets are protected from the beneficiary's creditors. The beneficiary's creditors cannot demand payment from the trustee.

Disadvantages to a Testamentary Trust

The several disadvantages to a testamentary trust are that:

(1) the trustee must provide an annual accounting to the court. The trustee must provide trust bank statements and receipts for every penny coming in and every penny going out of the trust. There are no exceptions. Every accounting has a filing fee.

(2) assets to fund the testamentary trust are not immediately available to the trustee to spend on the beneficiary. The assets must first pass through the probate process. In Virginia, the minimum time for probate is six months. The executor must first wrap up the probate estate before the trustee can qualify with the probate clerk and receive the trust assets.

(3) the trustee must be bonded with surety. What this means is that before qualifying with the probate clerk as trustee, the trust must qualify for a bond with surety. The bond is like an insurance policy. If the trustee misuses the trust assets, the bond company will *replace* the trust assets and then seek reimbursement from the trustee. The trustee must have good credit, have never filed bankruptcy, and not been convicted of a felony to qualify for a bond with surety. There is an annual fee for the bond with surety.

(4) the beneficiary's assets and expenses are a matter of public record, and anyone can see what the beneficiary has in trust.

All of these disadvantages to the testamentary trust are not present in a living trust. Living trust assets are immediately available for the trustee to spend on the trust beneficiary, the trustee is only accountable to the beneficiary, there is no bond with surety expense, and the trust assets and expenses are totally private.

Where to Look For More Information About Trusts and Wills for Specific Issues

Chapter 7: Seniors: What is Essential For You to Know When Your Ship Gets Rusty for more information about how only a will can protect assets for a disabled spouse and even protect assets in such a way that the spouse can qualify for government benefits that would not be available if those assets were given directly to a disabled spouse.

Chapter 8: Adult Children with Problems: How to Keep Them Out of Shark Infested Waters for more information about what to do if a child has drug, alcohol, or gambling issues.

Chapter 9: Blended Families: Hidden Mistakes That Can Torpedo and Sink Your Family for more information about how to protect a spouse AND provide for children who are not joint.

Chapter 10: Young Beneficiaries: Perimeter Defenses Around Your Forces for more information on how assets can be managed for young heirs using a testamentary trust.

Chapter 11: Special Needs Family Members: Keeping Them Out of Harm's Way for more information about how to leave an inheritance without destroying eligibility for government benefits.

Chapter 12: Pets: Defending the Defenseless for more information about how to safeguard your pet's well-being when you are gone.

Chapter 13: Unmarried Partners: Ways to Set Your Own Course for more information about how to avoid the state's default rules.

CHAPTER 6

Disability: How to Prepare For the Possibility of Engine Damage

Ever since mankind staked out a cave, farm, home, and other assets, the question has been "What will happen to my assets when I am gone?" Even the Bible talks about a will in Hebrews. Now that people are living longer, the likelihood of disability during a lifetime has increased. Which leads us to the new question of "How will my assets be managed if I don't die but become mentally disabled?"

Myth About Mental Capacity Diminishing Over Time

We believe that someone will notice and identify signs of dementia and take the necessary steps to prepare for asset management. In reality, this is not what happens. Often, parents will be able to hide the signs of dementia from their children. Wives will compensate for declining husbands and vice versa. Children often don't live nearby and don't notice the subtle changes in a parent's behavior. Even if children do notice, they can be reluctant to do anything and don't really know what to do.

Mental Capacity Disappearing In an Instant

A person's mental capacity can change in an *instant* from a stroke, accident, or illness. I helped three adult children when their mother experienced diminished mental capacity after a car accident. She was in her mid-sixties and working part time as a teacher when a large piece of furniture fell off the truck in front of her car as she was driving down a highway. Their mother recovered from most of her physical injuries, but the accident affected her mental ability. She was fine one minute and not fine the next minute.

Cliff was ready to retire. His business was for sale and he had a buyer. Cliff and his wife, Susan, had a motor home, and their plan was to hit the road when he retired. One day, Susan wasn't feeling well. She fainted. Susan was standing on their ceramic tile floor in the kitchen when she fainted. When you faint, you don't catch yourself, so she hit her head pretty hard. Her brain damage from the fall is permanent. Susan's symptoms resemble dementia. She cannot be left alone for a minute. Both their lives changed in an instant. Susan did not have a General Power of Attorney. Now Susan can't sign a General Power of Attorney because she does not have the required mental capacity. It's too late.

Your Battleship: a General Power of Attorney

A battleship provides anti-aircraft, anti-submarine, and anti-ship measures. I chose a battleship because it is a very powerful and versatile ship, and a General Power of Attorney is a very powerful legal document. A General Power of Attorney gives the person you name in the document as your agent your permission to sign your name to legal documents such as checks, contracts, and deeds.

Specific Permission to Use Specific Powers

The power of attorney must specifically state every power you want to grant to the person you name, called your agent. You control how much authority your agent has in the General Power of Attorney by listing the powers your agent has permission to use. A broad statement in a General Power of Attorney that your agent has permission to take any action will not be acceptable. For example, to avoid liability, your bank will want to see the exact words that give permission to your agent to open a bank account, close a bank account, write checks on a bank account, get information about a bank account, and more.

The General Power of Attorney we prepare for clients is almost twenty pages long. Just think about all the financial legal actions you can do that you might want to give your agent permission to do for you. Examples are sell property, rent property, sign a tax return, manage investments, sign a contract for healthcare services, close a credit card account, sell a car, and more.

Choose Your Agent Carefully

You choose who will manage your assets using a General Power of Attorney. I advise clients to choose someone who gets things done, keeps good records, is reliable, and trustworthy. Sometimes the best person to be your agent is not your oldest child or the child who lives nearby, or even one of your children. You can change your choice of agent by revoking your current General Power of Attorney and signing a new one.

You will need to select at least one successor agent. Even though your successor agent is named in your General Power of Attorney, they will have no authority to act unless the first agent named has resigned or died. So if you name your spouse as your first agent and a child as your successor agent, the child will have no powers unless your spouse resigns or dies.

What is Fiduciary Duty and Why is it Important?

There are legal guidelines your agent has to follow, because an agent under a power of attorney is a fiduciary. The term fiduciary goes back to Roman law. The word fiduciary comes from the Latin word fiducia, meaning "trust." A fiduciary has the power and obligation to act for another. They need to be trustworthy, honest, and use good faith in their actions. A fiduciary has a duty of care, which is a requirement that a person act with caution, attention, and prudence that a reasonable person in the circumstances would use. A fiduciary is not required to be perfect. They can make mistakes, but their decisions need to be based on the reasonable person standard described in the duty of care. In addition to agents using a power of attorney, fiduciaries include business advisors, attorneys, administrators of estates, and bankers.

One of the concepts fiduciary duty includes is that *everything* your agent does has to be for your benefit and to be only in your best interest. Your agent is not to take any action they would benefit from unless the General Power of Attorney specifically gives permission. For example, normally an agent would not be allowed to give your assets away. Giving your assets away as gifts would be contrary to an agent's fiduciary duty. The law presumes that giving your assets away is not for your benefit. You might be wondering why you would want your agent to give away some of your assets. If you regularly tithe to your church or give to charitable organizations, you might want to permit your agent to continue giving those gifts in the same amounts that you have given in the past. If you regularly give birthday, Christmas, and anniversary gifts to family members, you might want to permit your agent to continue giving those gifts in the same amounts that you have given in the past. Giving permission to your agent to continue gifting if you become mentally incapacitated and can't do it yourself does not *require* them to gift. If your assets become limited, they would stop the making of gifts, just like you would.

I usually advise spouses to allow unlimited gifting to each other when acting as an agent. I know this concept sounds strange to spouses because you don't think of the transfer of assets between you as gifts. However, the law takes a different view when a spouse is acting as an agent. See Chapter 7 for more information on super powers for seniors, such as unlimited gifting between spouses.

When a General Power of Attorney is Activated

A General Power of Attorney can be immediately activated as soon as you sign it, or it can be activated when certain conditions are met. It is possible for your General Power of Attorney to be activated only if you become mentally incapacitated. If that is the case, the General Power of Attorney should include instructions on who decides if you have become mentally incapacitated, such as two physicians must agree in writing. In this case, before your agent would be able to act, they would have to present the two physicians' letters stating you are mentally incapacitated *before* they can use the General Power of Attorney.

No Ongoing Fees with a General Power of Attorney

There are no ongoing fees with a General Power of Attorney. State laws allow an agent to reimburse themselves from your assets if they pay for something for you with their own money. So if your agent buys an ad online to run in the newspaper to sell your car and uses their credit card, they can be reimbursed. This makes sense. You wouldn't want the person helping you as your agent to have to pay for anything they do for you. If they did have to pay out of their pocket, it would be a whole lot harder to find someone to act as your agent.

A General Power of Attorney Protects Your Agent

A General Power of Attorney protects your agent when they are signing legal documents on your behalf. By signing your name, your agent is protected from financial responsibility and liability. If your agent is signing your name to legal documents on your behalf, your agent is not assuming financial responsibility for your debts. Again, if your agent was required to assume personal financial liability when they signed a contract or promissory note on your behalf, you would be hard pressed to find anyone who would be your agent.

The following story illustrates what happens when a family member signs their own name instead of signing as an agent using a General Power of Attorney. Amy's mother was having surgery. Her daughter, Amy, signed all the hospital admittance forms for her mother using her own name. Her mother's hospital bill was $30,000 more than her insurance would pay. Amy's mother did not have the money to pay the $30,000 hospital bill. Oh no—the hospital came after Amy for the $30,000. Amy couldn't believe that she could be responsible for her mother's hospital bill and went to court to fight against payment. Amy lost in court. Now her pay is garnished every paycheck until the $30,000 is paid to the hospital. One of the documents Amy signed her name to was responsibility for payment. This is why the hospital won. This devastating blow to Amy's finances could have been avoided if her mother had a General Power of Attorney. If Amy was her agent, Amy could have had legal permission to sign her mother's name to the hospital's admittance forms. By signing her mother's name, Amy's mother would be responsible for her own debts, not Amy.

Asset Protection for You

A General Power of Attorney can protect your assets. I often see parents add a child's name to their bank accounts. Their reasoning is that they want the child to be able to write checks and pay their bills if something happens to them. Sounds reasonable, but there is a risky hidden problem with this solution. When you add a child's name to your bank account, they become a joint owner. Joint ownership is what enables your child to write checks. What you don't know is that having a child's name on the bank account makes any funds in that account available to the child's creditors. Don't protest that you would only name a responsible child to your bank account. Bad things happen to good people. Your child could have huge medical bills they cannot pay due to an illness or accident. Their creditors can reach into your bank account and <u>take it all, not just half</u>!

Beth had an ex-husband who was behind on child support. Beth went to the local government department to get help in collecting the back child support she was owed. The agency found a bank account in Florida with the ex-husband's name on it. The agency was able to remove the amount owed from this bank account because Beth's ex-husband's name was on the account. But wait! The other name on the account was the ex-husband's mother. Did the money in the bank account really belong to the ex-husband's mother? Doesn't matter, because the ex-husband's name was on the account.

The Mistake That Can Sink Your Battleship— General Power of Attorney

Maybe you already have a General Power of Attorney. A common mistake that I see in reviewing General Power of Attorneys that people have is there is only one person named as their agent. Often, spouses name each other and then stop. Naming only one person as your agent can spell disaster.

What if your sole agent dies and you have a mental incapacity that prevents you from signing another General Power of Attorney? You are out of luck! See below for the expensive alternative.

The Expensive Alternative if You Don't Have a General Power of Attorney

What if you don't have a battleship—General Power of Attorney—in your battlegroup? If you become mentally incapacitated, you cannot sign a General Power of Attorney. You must understand what you are signing. In that case, someone (we don't know who) would have to volunteer and petition a court judge to appoint them to act on your behalf.

Going to court is the only legal alternative for someone who does not have a General Power of Attorney and does not have the legal capacity to sign one. This legal procedure costs thousands of dollars and takes months to complete.

Only if you are determined by a judge to be mentally incapacitated would someone be appointed to manage your assets. Therefore, you would not have a say in who the judge picked to manage your assets, and you don't even have to be at the hearing. But wait, there's more! What you have in assets would be disclosed and available to anyone because the information is available in the public records. The person managing your assets has to be bonded for your financial security and must provide an annual accounting to the court. The annual accounting becomes public record and shows every penny coming in and every penny going out, including bank statements and receipts.

Everything I've said above ALSO applies to spouses. So if you became mentally incapacitated and have an IRA in your name, your spouse won't have access to the funds in your IRA. Don't protest that they are the beneficiary on your IRA so they will get it. A beneficiary only has access when you die and not before. The only way for a spouse or anyone to use funds in an asset in your name alone is with a General Power of Attorney or by going to court and being appointed by a judge to manage your assets.

But wait, there's more! Imagine your spouse has had a stroke resulting in mental incapacity. Now you have to do everything yourself. Managing the care of your spouse and your home is just too much, and you want to downsize into a condo. If your home is owned by you and your spouse, you are not going to be able to sell your home. Your spouse can't legally sign a deed due to their mental incapacity. You will have to petition the court and get permission from a judge to sell your home and manage your spouse's half of the proceeds from the sale of your home. The court does not care what you do with your half of the sale proceeds. The court does care what you do with your spouse's share of the sale proceeds. You will have to file annual accountings showing the court what you are doing with your spouse's money—bank statements and receipts. You can't spend any of that money on yourself. It doesn't matter how long you have been married!

All the aggravation described above can be completely avoided with a great General Power of Attorney with more than one agent listed.

Your Medical Ship: A Healthcare Power of Attorney

The mission of a medical ship in the battlegroup is to provide medical support for the service members. A medical ship is a floating mobile hospital. A Healthcare Power of Attorney names who you want to make medical decisions for your medical support if you are not able to make medical decisions yourself.

When a Healthcare Power of Attorney is Effective

The Fourteenth Amendment to the Constitution has been interpreted to include that only you can make healthcare decisions for yourself if you are able. The Healthcare Power of Attorney becomes effective only if you are unconscious, delirious, on heavy pain medications, or otherwise unable to think straight and unable to make a decision for yourself.

Who Should You Choose to Make Healthcare Decisions for You?

In a Healthcare Power of Attorney, you choose the agents to make healthcare decisions for you. Healthcare decisions include choosing a doctor, choosing a medical facility, and deciding on treatment. The best person to choose as your healthcare agent is someone who would make healthcare decisions like you would for yourself. Amanda chose her daughter instead of her husband, because Amanda thought her daughter was more likely to make medical decisions like she would for herself. You can change your mind, revoke your Healthcare Power of Attorney, and sign a new document to name different people as your agent to make your medical decisions for you.

What Happens if You Don't Have a Healthcare Power of Attorney?

What if you don't have a Healthcare Power of Attorney? In an emergency, a healthcare decision might need to be made immediately, so in Virginia, a law was passed to give someone legal authority to make a decision for you if you are not able. Your spouse is in first position, then children, then parents, then siblings, and so on to your next living blood relative. What if you don't want your estranged spouse or child to be responsible to make medical decisions for you? When you have a Healthcare Power of Attorney, you don't have to follow your state's list and can name anyone you want. You get to have it your way.

Your Minesweeper: a Living Will

A minesweeper's mission is defensive. This ship clears the path of unseen underwater mines so the battlegroup can proceed safely. Having a Living Will can clear the way for your loved ones during a very difficult time.

Your Decision Rules!

A Living Will does not grant authority to anyone or name anyone to do something for you. Instead, it makes your decisions known to your loved ones so they don't have to decide. A Living Will is your statement about what you do and do not want if you are near the end of life, in a coma, or in a persistent vegetative state. Near the end of life is defined as having a terminal condition and in the last few months of life. The Living Will states whether or not you want your life prolonged with procedures such as a ventilator, feeding tube, or an IV for hydration. A Living Will can give permission for pain medication, even though the dose may shorten your life.

When a Living Will Takes Effect

The conditions for a Living Will to take effect are not immediate. Doctors will run tests to make a determination on your condition first. Another condition for the Living Will to take effect is if you are unable to make the decision for yourself because you are unconscious or receiving a lot of pain medication and can't think straight. You call the shots as long as you are able.

Don't Make Your Family Decide

A huge benefit of having a written Living Will is that it removes the decision-making burden from your loved ones. All your family needs to do is read your Living Will. There is a difference between talking about what you want and putting what you want in writing. If you just talk about what you would want, your family will not know for sure. What if you changed your mind since the last time you spoke about your end of life decision? In some cases when there is not a Living Will, a doctor may require that all family members agree on what to do or not do. This puts one family member in the position of having the ability to veto everyone else. One veto by a family member means that the doctor will not end life support. I've had adult children tell me that making this decision for a parent was the hardest decision they ever had to make. Some children tell me that to this day they wonder if they made the right decision. I know this nightmare is not what you want for your children or other family members.

Susan has four siblings. Their elderly mother fell down a flight of stairs and was very badly injured. Their mother was put on life support while the doctors determined the extent of her injuries. Finally, her doctor told her children that their mother was dependent on the life support and asked—did they want the life support to continue? Susan's mother did not have a Living Will. The doctor explained that all five children would have to agree before he could discontinue the life support. What if one of the children couldn't make a decision? Their mother would have continued on life support indefinitely at a cost of thousands of dollars a month. What would their mother have wanted? Susan's mother could have prevented forcing her children to make this difficult decision for her if she had a Living Will.

Advance Medical Directive

You may see the term Advance Medical Directive. An Advance Medical Directive is an umbrella term that includes both the Healthcare Power of Attorney and a Living Will in one document.

Personalized, not Standardized, Living Will

You can provide specific guidance in your Living Will if it is not just a form and is prepared just for you. Guidance can include a definition of what you consider life prolonging procedures. Specific guidelines concerning religious beliefs can be specified in a Living Will. For example, Jehovah's Witness followers are not allowed to have blood transfusions.

If you have a Virginia Advanced Medical Directive form that you filled out at the hospital, read it very carefully. A section of an Advanced Directive is a Living Will. I've read some that apply only if you have a terminal condition. A coma or permanent vegetative state is not a terminal condition. Therefore, if your document states terminal condition, your Living Will won't apply for anything else and it will be just as if you didn't have one, resulting in no guidance for your loved ones.

What Is A Do Not Resuscitate Order?

A Living Will and a Do Not Resuscitate Order have different purposes. A Do Not Resuscitate Order is a decision made ahead of time to not revive you under certain conditions. An attorney cannot prepare a Do Not Resuscitate Order for you. A doctor has to prepare and sign that form.

Your Communications Ship:
Authorization to Release Protected
Health Information

Long ago, ships communicated with flags and lanterns. Today, communications between ships is very sophisticated. The communications ship in the battlegroup is responsible for transmitting information from the highest ranking officer in the battlegroup to all the other ships.

An Authorization to Release Protected Health Information is the communications ship in your battlegroup. Congress passed laws to protect the unauthorized disclosure of your health information. These laws are commonly known as HIPPA laws. The limitations on disclosure of health information even includes spouses. If you see your doctor for tests, your spouse cannot get the results of those tests from your doctor unless you give permission to your doctor to share the information with your spouse.

Why the HIPPA Form at Your Doctor's Office is Not Sufficient

Some doctors will have their own form at their office so you can name the people they have permission to share your health information with. That form stays at your doctor's office. What if you are in a car accident and are taken to an emergency room? If you are conscious, you can name the people the doctors can talk to about your condition. If you are unconscious, the doctors will only share information about your medical condition with the person you named as your agent on your Healthcare Power of Attorney or who the state statute names as your healthcare decision maker. So if your medical decision maker is your spouse and you are unconscious, your doctor legally won't be able to provide your medical information to other family members, such as your children, siblings, and close friends.

Effective for Any Doctor

The advantage of having the Authorization to Release Protected Health Information document is that it is effective for any doctor at any time. You can list anyone you want on your release, including friends, in addition to family. A doctor just needs one copy of a release to have permission to talk to anyone listed on the release. Remember that the release gives access to information only—not medical decision-making authority.

Declassified Secret #4

Hidden rough seas exist that can throw your estate plan off course.

Chapters 7–13 will be a must read depending on your situation. So feel free to pick and choose or skip altogether.

Chapter 7: Seniors: What is Essential For You to Know When Your Ship Gets Rusty

Chapter 7 is what is essential for seniors. If you are not a senior but have parents who are seniors, you can read this chapter for them or show it to them. You must read Chapters 5 and 6 to understand this chapter.

Chapter 8: Adult Children with Problems: How to Keep Them Out of Shark Infested Waters

Chapter 8 is for parents who have adult children with problems such as an unstable marriage, poor money management resulting in debts, or alcohol or drug issues. Leaving an inheritance to them outright could cause a disaster.

Chapter 9: Blended Families: Hidden Mistakes That Can Torpedo and Sink Your Family

Chapter 9 is for couples who have children from a previous relationship. There are so many things that can go wrong, this is a precarious situation for the surviving spouse and the deceased spouse's children.

Chapter 10: Younger Beneficiaries: Perimeter Defenses Around Your Forces

Chapter 10 is for parents with minor children. This chapter discusses asset management for children as well as naming a potential guardian to raise your children. If you are a grandparent, read this chapter and then show it to your kids with minor children.

Chapter 11: Special Needs Family Members: Keeping Them Out of Harm's Way

Chapter 11 is for parents of special needs children AND husbands and wives who have mentally incapacitated spouses. A must read also if you have a parent with a mental incapacity.

Chapter 12: Pets: Defending the Defenseless

Chapter 12 is for parents of pets. Read this if you care about what happens to your pet if you become mentally incapacitated, in addition to what happens to your pet when you die.

Chapter 13: Unmarried Partners: Ways to Set Your Own Course

Chapter 13 is for unmarried partners. If this is not you, you can skip this chapter.

CHAPTER 7

Seniors: What is Essential For You to Know When Your Ship Gets Rusty

When navy ships are commissioned, the paint on the ship is new and everything looks fresh. The navy takes very good care of every ship, but over time, things just naturally change. In addition to material changes, the missions of the navy can also change. Changes in the navy mission can result in changes in ships.

Over time, you will experience changes in your mental and physical condition. These changes point to a need for changes in your estate planning documents. The estate planning document that will need to be reviewed and updated when you become a senior is your battleship—a General Power of Attorney.

Your Battleship: a General Power of Attorney

Seniors need to have "super powers" granted to their agent in a General Power of Attorney. If you see or have seen an attorney who does not know about long-term care planning, that attorney just won't know about these additional powers that are unique to seniors. So if you are a senior and have a standard General Power of Attorney, your document won't have the super powers your agent might need if your physical or mental health declines and you need additional care.

Why Allowing Your Agent to Benefit is an Unusual Super Power

When someone is acting as your agent, by law, they are not allowed to personally benefit from any actions taken on your behalf. When a spouse is acting as your agent, they also are bound by fiduciary duty. You can overcome the fiduciary duty limitations in your General Power of Attorney by specifically giving permission for your agent to benefit in certain situations that you specify in the General Power of Attorney. Refer to Chapter 6 for a more complete explanation about fiduciary duty.

Giving Your Spouse the Unlimited Gifting Permission Senior Super Power

You can give your spouse unlimited gifting permission in your General Power of Attorney. For couples who have been married a long time, this seems like a strange idea, but read on to see why this gifting power is critical to your estate plan. Normally, an agent would be prohibited from using their power as your agent to gift to themselves (even if your agent is your spouse). The most common reason for giving unlimited gifting permission to your spouse as your agent is to transfer complete home ownership to your spouse. Most married couples own their home jointly with survivorship. This means that when one spouse dies, the home immediately belongs to the surviving spouse. But what if your spouse has dementia? If you die first, your home would instantly belong to your surviving spouse. Because the surviving spouse has dementia, they would be unable to sign a deed to sell the home because they would not have the required legal capacity. If the surviving spouse with dementia does not have a General Power of Attorney giving authority to an agent to sell the home, they have a problem. The only solution in this case is for someone to go to court to be appointed as a conservator and ask for a judge's permission to sell the home on behalf of the person with dementia. When there is court involvement, the process will take time and be expensive. See Chapter 6 for more information on the conservatorship process.

Evelyn asked me to review her estate plan because her husband Ben has dementia. Their daughter, Lucy, and their grandson live with them. When I described the following scenario, Evelyn was horrified. If Evelyn were to die first, their home would automatically belong to Ben because they are joint owners with survivorship. If Ben needs nursing home care, the home would have to be sold and the proceeds used only for his care. This means that Lucy and their grandson would be homeless, without any money. Lucy has disabilities that prevent her from working. This situation would be disastrous.

Evelyn and her husband Ben already had their estate planning documents. That was a significant benefit, because now that Ben has dementia, he can't sign any legal documents. The even bigger benefit was that his General Power of Attorney allowed Evelyn as his agent to have unlimited gifting permission to herself. Unlimited gifting to herself means that she could transfer assets from her husband to herself.

Spouses don't think anything of giving each other gifts. What makes this different is that Evelyn would be acting as Ben's agent when making gifts to herself. Ben's General Power of Attorney must specify that Evelyn has permission to make unlimited gifts to herself.

So here is the new estate plan that we created for Evelyn. She signed her name and Ben's name to a deed to transfer ownership of their home to just Evelyn. Ben's General Power of Attorney had to be recorded along with the deed to show that Evelyn had legal permission from Ben. Then Evelyn signed a new will that gives their home to their daughter, Lucy. Now if Evelyn dies before Ben, their home will be owned by Lucy. Lucy and her son already live with Ben and Evelyn, so she will be able to care for Ben as long as possible. If Ben needs nursing home care, the home will not have to be sold and the proceeds used to pay for Ben's care.

A few weeks later, I was meeting with Sharon to review her estate plan. Sharon's husband also has dementia. However in his case, his General Power of Attorney did not allow any gifting. So I had to tell Sharon there was very little we could do, because her husband couldn't sign any legal documents.

There is a special way to provide asset protection for a spouse with dementia that is covered in <u>Chapter 11: Special Needs Family Members: Keeping Them Out of Harm's Way</u>.

Payment for Your Care Senior Super Power

Another senior super power is to give permission to a child when acting as your agent to pay themselves for your care. In this case, a child might be taking care of you in your home or in their home. The general fiduciary duty rules wouldn't allow them to pay themselves if they are caring for you. If you give permission for a child as your agent to pay themselves for your care, it doesn't mean that they *have* to pay themselves. It just means that they have permission.

The reason you should consider this permission is that it is currently an effective way to transfer money from your estate to a child without triggering a penalty if you later apply for government benefits. For example, if you give money to a child, the gift will trigger a period of ineligibility for Medicaid benefits. If you pay a child to take care of you, there is no gift because you are receiving a valuable service. The difference is that a child cannot pay themselves if they are also your agent unless you have clearly given permission in your General Power of Attorney.

Home Improvements to Agent's Home Senior Super Power

Allowing your child as your agent to use your money to make home improvements in their home if you are staying with them is another senior super power you can give permission for in your General Power of Attorney. The home improvements can be a wheelchair ramp, renovating a bathroom so it is handicap accessible, or even adding a room to their home for you to stay in. Although all the examples are for your benefit since you will be staying with that child, they would benefit too. Going back to the broad fiduciary duty rules, a child is not allowed to benefit when acting as your agent. In the examples given, a child would also be benefiting, so they would need permission in the General Power of Attorney.

CHAPTER 8

Adult Children with Problems: How to Keep Them Out of Shark Infested Waters

The navy goes overboard with training for every possible disaster. My first experience with disaster training was at officer candidate school. The instructors divided us into small groups for damage control training. We went into a simulator that looked like a compartment (room) in a ship, but this compartment could produce water leaks in various places, such as pipes. Our job was to patch the leaks. Cold water came pouring in from numerous holes. The space we were in began to fill up with water. As the shortest person on the team, I had a lot of incentive to help. The instructors would not turn the water off until we patched the leaks. It was exciting, and we got hands on experience in what we should do.

You can perform your own damage control with a properly prepared estate plan. You trained your kids to make good decisions and handle money wisely, but even though kids are raised right, they sometimes just don't do right. Perhaps money runs through their hands like sand or they have a drug or alcohol abuse or gambling problem. What's a parent to do?

Why Disinheriting Children Is Not the Only Solution

Sometimes parents will disinherit children with these problems. After all, their inheritance will be gone in just a few months, or worse still, the money will support their gambling, drug, or alcohol problem. Sometimes parents will leave the problem child's share to a responsible child with the understanding that they are to use the additional inheritance for the care of the problem child. Giving the additional money to the responsible child is risky. What if the responsible child has huge medical bills, is divorced by their spouse, someone sues them, or they need nursing home care? From the outside looking in, the additional inheritance money appears to belong to the responsible child. That additional money held for the problem child will be subject to loss if something bad happens to the responsible child. For example, if the responsible child dies, all of their assets will transfer to their beneficiary and heirs. The problem child's inheritance can disappear through no fault of the responsible child.

Why the Total Protection Solution Is the Way to Go

You can leave an inheritance for a problem child in a way that is totally protected from loss and can be used *only for their benefit*. The key to this solution is to hold their inheritance in a living trust or a testamentary trust created by your will for the benefit of the problem child. In both cases, you decide the rules for distribution for the benefit of the problem child. Their inheritance can ensure that they have medical and dental care, food, and even a roof over their head when you are gone. The problem child's inheritance can be protected from their creditors and their divorce settlement.

It's even possible to word the trust so the child can get their inheritance outright if they stop their gambling or abusing drugs or alcohol. Their inheritance could become a reward after a lasting change in their behavior.

What Doesn't Work

What won't work is requiring a child to do something to keep their inheritance after you are gone. Ed and Cathy have three children. Their oldest, Charles, had never been good at managing money. Money just slipped through his fingers. Charles had lived at home with Ed and Cathy for the past twenty-five years. Cathy wanted to leave their home to Charles and their daughter Emily on the condition that Charles pay his share of the homeowner's insurance and taxes. If Charles did not pay his share, he would have to move out.

Ed was against passing ownership to include Charles because he said that Charles would be unlikely to be able to pay his share of the insurance and tax payments. In reality, the burden of paying the insurance and taxes would be placed on Emily. If Emily got mad and didn't want to pay because Charles refused to pay his share, their home would be lost to pay back taxes.

I pointed out to them that once Charles received ownership through their will, there was no way to take it back. Emily would be unable to evict her brother for nonpayment of insurance and taxes, because Charles would be a joint owner with her. What Ed and Cathy were trying to achieve was not possible with a will.

It's important for an estate planning attorney to understand probate so they know what is and is not possible. I could write anything in your will and it will only come to light after you are gone that what you wanted is not possible in the probate system. This is why you need an estate planning attorney with experience in probate.

A living trust could have accomplished Ed and Cathy's goal of holding the home and letting Charles and Emily live in it. The living trust would pay the insurance and taxes. The living trust rules could state that when the trust money ran out, the home would be sold. An alternative would be to have the executor sell their home, divide the assets, and have a testamentary trustee hold Charles's share in trust, keeping control of the money for Charles's benefit, but not giving him the money outright. Ed and Cathy agreed that Charles would drive the testamentary trustee crazy, so that was not a good solution for them.

This is an excellent example of why estate planning is collaborative. We know the law, and you know your family. Together, we craft a solution that is just right for you and your situation.

CHAPTER 9

Blended Families: Hidden Mistakes That Can Torpedo and Sink Your Family

I was a student at the Navy Postgraduate School in Monterey, California for eighteen months. The title of my curriculum was Joint Command, Control, and Communications. I learned that each of the military branches, navy, marine corps, air force, and army, have their own way of viewing operations and communication. It starts with different terminology for the same thing. For the navy, securing a building means locking it up. For the marine corps, securing a building means taking control of it. For the army, securing a building means posting guards around the building. One way the military services try to get past the difficulties in working together is to practice using war games. No one gets hurt, and problems come to the surface for attention.

It is not unusual for someone to remarry after the loss of a spouse or a divorce. A blended family results when two people marry and one or both have children from a previous marriage. Estate planning is especially important for the blended family. War games are the military's way of discovering unseen problems that if left alone would cause bigger problems in the future. Blended families don't get to pretend that someone has died to see what happens to the family. Sometimes family problems and long held grudges don't come to light until a parent dies. Then it can get really ugly and expensive.

Patty thought her relationship with her husband's two children was just fine. She found out differently on the day of her husband Hank's funeral. Hank's daughter came to her house after the funeral and proceeded to voice a list of grievances she had against her stepmother, Patty. Evidently, Hank's daughter cooperated as long as he was alive, but now that her dad was gone, she was angry. Unfortunately, Hank had named both Patty and his daughter as co-executors. Patty's stepdaughter did everything she could to frustrate and make Patty miserable. By the time Patty came to see me, she was in tears. Acting as co-executors was not going to work for Patty. We went to court to get a judge's permission to release her as co-executor of her husband's estate, and I became the buffer between Patty and her stepdaughter. The stepdaughter's hidden resentment against Patty resulted in a lot of heartache, stress, frustration, and expense for Patty. It all could have been prevented with a personalized estate plan for blended families.

If you answer yes to any of the three questions below, it is critical for you to plan ahead to protect your children's inheritance:

1. Do I or my spouse have children that are not ours together?

2. Do I want to make sure that my children get something when I am gone?

3. Do I want to protect my spouse financially and protect my children's inheritance too?

Accidentally Disinheriting Your Children

It is possible for your will to leave everything to your children, but they get nothing when you die. A client asked me about that exact situation. He said that his friend, Frank, had remarried after Frank's wife died. The client asked me why Frank's children didn't get anything when Frank died. How could that happen? If Frank listed his spouse as the beneficiary of an asset such as an IRA, and they had joint bank accounts, the spouse would get the IRA and the bank accounts automatically. We will never know if Frank unintentionally disinherited his children. He probably was just unaware of what would happen.

A will only controls an asset in your name alone, with no beneficiary. Assets owned by both husband and wife together automatically belong to the survivor. If the house is titled in the husband and wife's names, with right of survivorship, the house immediately belongs to the survivor, and the deceased spouse's children don't get the house. The survivor's will controls what will happen to the house when the survivor dies. See Chapter 5 for a review on wills.

Blended Family Solutions

There are estate planning solutions that will safely preserve your assets after your death for your spouse's use if they need financial help, and then at your spouse's death, be distributed to your children. But you have to make these plans in advance using a carefully prepared estate plan.

Using wills to accomplish a blended family's estate plan has a serious risk that you need to consider. Husband and wife can have wills that state everything goes to the survivor and then when the survivor dies everything is divided among his children and her children equally. Next, the husband dies, and everything now belongs to the wife. There is nothing to prevent the wife from changing her will and leaving everything to her children. The huge risk is that the survivor will change their mind.

A living trust is the absolute best estate planning solution for blended families. The living trust rules can state that when the husband or wife dies, the trust rules cannot be changed. Therefore, all the children will still be beneficiaries when the survivor dies.

A living trust is also more flexible than a will. Tom owned his home and had two adult children before he married Vickie. Tom can state in his living trust that Vickie can stay in the home as long as she wants, for one year, or for whatever time period Tom wants. Then when Vickie moves out, the trust rules can state that ownership of the home shall be transferred to Tom's children. The trust rules can state that if Vickie remarries or moves a male person into the home, she must move out. You can have it your way with a living trust. A Last Will & Testament is not as flexible and won't work.

It is possible for living trust rules to state that a portion of trust assets will belong to the surviving spouse and a portion of trust assets will be separately held for the future benefit of the deceased spouse's children. This way, if the surviving spouse runs out of money, the trustee can dip into the children's share if necessary. When the surviving spouse dies, the deceased spouse's children receive their inheritance. See Chapter 5 for an in-depth explanation of a living trust.

The solutions provided above are just examples. A lot more is possible. It just depends on your situation and what your goals are. This is why communication between us is so important.

CHAPTER 10

Younger Beneficiaries: Perimeter Defenses Around Your Forces

When a navy battlegroup deploys, there are ships and submarines that surround the group of ships to act as the perimeter defense. The same principle applies in the air. Fighter jets will surround the more vulnerable refueling planes for their defense.

None of us can predict how or when we will die. It is possible for your estate plan to establish a perimeter defense around your younger children or grandchildren's inheritance in addition to naming your choice of who would raise your children if you cannot. High profile situations such as Michael Jackson's, Anna Nichole Smith's, Keith Ledger's, and Seymour Hoffman's deaths remind parents that legal planning must be done to ensure their children do not wind up with a court-appointed guardian who might not be their choice, and that plans are in place for the management of their children's inheritance.

Ask yourself two simple questions:

1. What would happen to my children if something happened to me?

2. Would someone have immediate access to my assets for the care of my children if something happened to me?

Naming a Prospective Guardian

If you (or your adult children) don't make the decision about who would raise your minor children (or grandchildren), you will be leaving that decision to a judge who doesn't know your family. Your family's defenses will be down, and an outsider—a judge—will decide, without knowing anything about you and what you would want.

Virginia parents of a one-year-old child went out on a date night and never came home. They were both killed in a car accident. Both sets of grandparents wanted to raise their grandson. Because the parents did not have wills, a judge decided the fate of the little boy. In my opinion, the judge decided not to decide. Instead, both sets of grandparents have joint legal custody of their grandson. One week he is with his mom's parents, and the next week he is with his dad's parents. Is that what the child's parents would have wanted? We will never know because neither of them had a will.

A will is the only way in Virginia to name a prospective guardian for minor children. Your will gives you a voice in court as to your choice of who you want to raise your children if you can't. If you don't have a will naming prospective guardians, you don't have a voice.

Inheritance Management: What Can Go Wrong

The state law in Virginia is that a minor cannot directly receive their inheritance. Instead, inheritance assets are managed by the guardian of the minor's estate, under court supervision, until the minor's eighteenth birthday. The guardian of the minor's estate is usually a family member, and in Virginia, a parent is the first choice. The guardian of the minor's estate has limits on the amount of inheritance assets that can be spent on the minor each year. The guardian of the minor's estate must provide an annual accounting to the court with bank statements and receipts. On the minor's eighteenth birthday, any remaining inheritance assets must be turned over to the beneficiary. The annual accountings clearly show what the beneficiary will receive outright on their eighteenth birthday. Anyone can see what the beneficiary will receive. This is the worst possible plan, because most young adults don't have any experience in managing money, can fall prey to greedy friends, and generally make poor decisions on what to do with their inheritance.

I met with a mother, Brenda, who had a seventeen-year-old son, Eric. Brenda and Eric's father were divorced. Eric's father had a $100,000 life insurance policy that named Eric as the beneficiary. Eric's father died. Brenda asked me if it was possible to prevent turning over the $100,000 to Eric on his eighteenth birthday. Eric was looking at very expensive cars, and Brenda was afraid Eric would spend most, if not all, of the $100,000 on a car. Eric's decision to spend money on a hot car is not surprising, because he is inexperienced in handling large sums of money. Unfortunately, I had to tell Brenda that she would have to give all $100,000 to Eric on his eighteenth birthday. It was too late to do any planning. In this case, Eric's father's gift was probably going to do more harm than good. It didn't have to be that way.

Inheritance Management Solutions

A testamentary trust or a living trust is the way to manage and protect assets for a younger beneficiary. See Chapter 5 for more details about a testamentary trust created by a will.

A Testamentary Younger Beneficiary Trust Solution

A trust created by a will is called a testamentary younger beneficiary trust. It is created only if the conditions specified in the will are met. A will can state that if any beneficiary is under the age of, say, twenty-four (you get to pick the age), their inheritance will be held for them and managed by a trustee (you get to pick the trustee) until their twenty-fourth birthday.

Inheritance assets managed by a testamentary younger beneficiary trust can be spent on the younger beneficiary by the trustee. There are no limitations on how much per year can be spent on the younger beneficiary. The trustee, who is older, wiser, and experienced with money management, makes the decisions on how the trust assets will be spent for the benefit of the younger beneficiary. The will can be written to make the inheritance available for health, maintenance, and welfare of the beneficiary. This is very broad and means that the trustee can use the assets for just about anything, such as school tuition, rent, food, down payment on a home, a wedding, medical, and much more. The court monitors how the trustee is managing the beneficiary's money by requiring an annual accounting. Then at the age specified in the will, the trustee would turn over any money remaining in the testamentary trust outright to the beneficiary.

I met with a mother, Susan, who wanted to make sure that her daughter, Emily, would receive an inheritance from her. Emily was a child from her first marriage. Now Susan was married again, and had a son from her second marriage. Susan and her husband owned all their assets jointly. If Susan died first, all assets would automatically be owned by her second husband. Her goal was peace of mind in the event she died, he remarried after her death, and all assets went to the new wife. She wanted to know with certainty that Emily would receive an inheritance from her.

The plan we created for Susan was for her to purchase a life insurance policy naming her estate as her beneficiary. By naming her estate as the beneficiary, Susan's will would control what happened to the proceeds from the life insurance policy. Susan's will said that her estate beneficiary would be Emily, but if she was younger than twenty-three years of age, her inheritance would be held for her in a younger beneficiary trust. Susan named her husband as the trustee, giving him the authority to manage Emily's inheritance for her, but under court supervision. Based on Susan's budget, this estate plan fit her goal perfectly. Susan sighed with relief when her estate plan was in place. Susan knew exactly how things would turn out for her daughter if something happened to her.

A disadvantage to a testamentary younger beneficiary trust is that the assets will not be immediately available to spend on the younger beneficiary. Since the asset is controlled by a will, it has to proceed through the probate process before the asset is transferred to the trustee. In Virginia, an estate can't be closed until six months have passed. When the estate is closed, the trustee assumes control of the younger beneficiary's inheritance.

A Living Trust Solution

A living trust is the alternative to a will. See Chapter 5 for the basics of a living trust. The living trust rules can state that if a beneficiary is under a specified age (the grantors decide the age), then the successor trustee (grantors pick who will be their successor trustee) is to keep the beneficiary's inheritance in the trust instead of distributing the inheritance outright.

The trust can be written to give instructions to the successor trustee to spend the inheritance on the younger beneficiary for the health, maintenance, and welfare of the beneficiary. This is very broad, and means that the successor trustee can use the trust assets for just about anything, such as school tuition, rent, food, down payment on a home, a wedding, medical, and much more. The trustee is older, wiser, and experienced with money, so they make the decisions on how the inheritance will be spent for the benefit of the beneficiary. With a living trust, there is no court involvement. The trust funds are *immediately* available to the successor trustee for whatever the beneficiary needs. The trustee will need to keep a record of the beneficiary's asset income and expenses, but that information is kept private from the public.

At the age specified in the trust rules, the successor trustee would distribute the younger beneficiary's inheritance to them outright and free of the trust. Another alternative can be to have the trust rules state that the younger beneficiary can become the trustee of their inheritance and keep their assets in the trust. The trust rules can state that any assets still controlled by the trust would pass to the beneficiary's children at the beneficiary's death. The significant advantage to this solution is that the beneficiary's trust assets would not become a part of their estate. What this means is that the beneficiary's spouse would not receive the trust assets, but instead the beneficiary's children would receive the assets. In some family situations, this advantage is significant.

CHAPTER 11

Special Needs Family Members: Keeping Them out of Harm's Way

Long ago, the purpose of a lighthouse was to protect assets. The lighthouse warned ships carrying valuable assets away from dangerous waters. There are ways to protect assets for family members who can't manage assets themselves due to illness, dementia, or physical limitations. There are three possibilities:

(1) a special needs trust created by a will is possible for spouses,

(2) a special needs trust created by a will is possible for parents and grandparents of a special needs child or grandchild, and

(3) a special needs trust created by a trust agreement.

I want to clarify right away that a regular revocable living trust in most cases will be viewed as an available asset, and will prevent a beneficiary from qualifying for government benefits like Medicaid. The law says that if a beneficiary has access to assets or can demand payment, then those assets should be used for the beneficiary's care. The exception to the rule is a special needs trust (also called a supplemental needs trust).

A Lighthouse for Your Spouse

Most married couples have "I love you" wills. An "I love you" will says that I love you so much, I leave everything to you. The following true story describes why an "I love you" will is not always the best plan for everyone.

A man named Bill took care of his invalid wife, Karen. Bill's health was beginning to decline. He worried about what would happen to Karen if something happened to him. I explained that with his "I love you" will, everything would go to Karen. Karen also had dementia, so she wouldn't be able to manage any assets if something happened to Bill. Due to the level of care Karen needed, she would have to move to a nursing home if Bill couldn't take care of her. Their home would be sold and all of their money spent at thousands of dollars a month on nursing home care until it was all gone.

Happily, I could tell Bill that there was a better plan available. The solution safeguards almost all their assets for Karen's benefit AND almost immediately qualifies her for Medicaid benefits. Wow!

We prepared a new will for Bill that leaves everything for Karen's benefit, but is protected for her in a special needs trust. Then we transferred the majority of their assets into Bill's name alone with no beneficiary listed. To be controlled by Bill's will, an asset had to be in Bill's name alone. If an asset like a bank account was in both his name and Karen's name, then the funds in the bank account would automatically belong to Karen if Bill died first. Because the majority of their assets were now in Bill's name alone, his will would control what happened to the asset if he died.

Now if Bill dies first, Karen would move to a nursing home, and because she has few assets, she would qualify for the government Medicaid benefit after paying the nursing home for a few months with her few assets. Medicaid would pay the cost of her nursing home care.

The special needs trust would pay for benefits that enable Karen to have a better quality of life. For example, the special needs trust can pay the difference to upgrade her to a private room at the nursing home, pay for a geriatric care manager to make sure that Karen is receiving the best care, pay for flowers to be delivered to her room each week, pay for eyeglasses and dental care, and much more. Then at Karen's death, whatever is left in her trust will be distributed to their heirs.

You can imagine how relieved Bill was with this plan. He knew that if he was not around to care for Karen, their money would be able to keep her quality of life as high as possible. Now he had peace of mind, knowing there was a plan for taking care of Karen.

In fact, Bill did become ill and die before Karen. Their daughter was very relieved to know that she would have money available to provide her mother with as high a quality of life as possible for the rest of her mother's days.

The law is quirky. A married couple cannot create a special needs trust for each other in a revocable living trust. A special needs trust for a spouse can only be created by a will.

A Lighthouse for Your Special Needs Child

Parents used to disinherit a disabled child. It sounds harsh, but if a child receives an inheritance, it usually disqualifies them from receiving government benefits. Most of the time, the Medicaid benefit for health care is critical for special needs children. Sometimes parents will leave the disabled child's share to a responsible child with the understanding that they are to use the additional inheritance for the care of the disabled child.

Giving the additional money to the responsible child is risky. What if the responsible child has huge medical bills, is divorced by their spouse, someone sues them, or they need nursing home care? From the outside looking in, the additional inheritance money appears to belong to the responsible child. That additional money held for the disabled child will be subject to loss if something bad happens to the responsible child. For example, if the responsible child dies, all of their assets will transfer to their beneficiary and heirs. The disabled child's inheritance can disappear through no fault of the responsible child.

There is a better, safer solution. That solution is a special needs trust (sometimes called a supplemental needs trust). There are three ways parents and grandparents can create a special needs trust for a child or grandchild. A special needs trust can be created by a will or by a trust.

The first method to consider is a stand-alone special needs trust if you think other family members will want to contribute to the special needs trust. The grantor would create a separate living trust. The grantor would be a parent or grandparent. The grantor can also be the trustee. The beneficiary of the trust would be the disabled child or grandchild. Now the trust exists as a legal entity. Because the trust is a legal entity, the trust can be named as the beneficiary on a life insurance policy, bank account, investment account, or just about any asset. The trust can even be named as a beneficiary in a will or a different trust.

Tom and Betty have three children. Alex is physically disabled and will never be able to work. Tom and Betty establish a separate special needs trust. They are the grantors and trustees of the trust, and Alex is the beneficiary. Tom and Betty designate some of their assets to be distributed to the trust for Alex by naming the accounts to transfer on death to the special needs trust. When both Tom and Betty are deceased, the successor trustee will use a death certificate to transfer the payable on death accounts to the special needs trust. The funds will be available almost immediately for Alex's benefit without disrupting his government benefits. Other family members and friends can also name Alex's special needs trust as their beneficiary. If another family dies before Tom and Betty, there won't be any problems leaving funds to Alex's special needs trust, because it already exists as a legal entity.

The second method to consider is having a regular revocable living trust. The trust rules can state that when Tom and Betty are deceased, the trust assets will be divided into thirds, one-third distributed to each child. However, Alex's one-third will be held in a special needs trust. So it is a trust within a trust. Funds for Alex will be available immediately and will not disrupt any government benefits that Alex is receiving. The only disadvantage to this solution is that other family members and friends can't make a contribution to Alex's special needs trust.

The third solution is to use a will. Tom and Betty would state in their wills that the one-third left for Alex will be held in a special needs trust created by their will. A special needs trust created by a will still safeguards the assets left for Alex and will not disrupt any government benefits that he will receive. But there are two disadvantages to this solution. First, Alex's inheritance will need to pass through the probate system. Therefore the assets will not be available immediately to fund the special needs trust. Second is that because the special needs trust does not exist until both Tom and Betty are gone, other family members or friends will not be able to contribute to Alex's special needs trust.

All three possible solutions need to be considered and planned in advance. Once Tom and Betty are deceased, it will be too late.

CHAPTER 12

Pets: Defending the Defenseless

As you know, our navy not only protects our homeland, but also protects and defends other countries and people who do not have the resources we do. It is possible in many states, including Virginia, to provide for your pet while you are living but mentally incapacitated and after you are gone.

Imagine that you are in an accident on your way home and are injured. What if your spouse is out of town when you are taken to the emergency room? What if you are unconscious? What if your pets are in crates waiting for you to come home, let them out, and feed them?

Americans spend over $41 billion annually on pet care. Yet many pet owners forget to provide for their companions if they are injured or die.

While You are Alive

First, every pet owner needs to have and carry an Emergency Pet Alert Card to alert medical providers that they have pets. The card should list the names and telephone numbers of their pet emergency caregivers. Pet owners also need to prepare written instructions outlining how your pets should be cared for, including the name, address, and telephone of their veterinarian and any medications the pet is receiving.

Second, you want to examine your General Power of Attorney to see if permission to spend your money on your pet is specifically stated. If not, your agent will not have legal permission to pay for pet care with your assets. It sounds crazy, but it's true. There is even a court case in California about this issue. The legal rationale comes back to fiduciary duty. (For a review of fiduciary duty, see Chapter 6.) Your agent can only spend your money on you. You don't see a veterinarian for healthcare or eat pet food. So you need to give permission for those payments in your General Power of Attorney.

When You are Gone

What about when you are gone? The law has long considered a pet to be personal property, like a chair. It wouldn't make sense to leave assets for the benefit of a chair. But the law has caught up with the special way that we think about our pets.

Virginia allows pet trusts. This means you can leave funds in a trust that can only be used for your pet's care. If you just leave money directly to someone for the care of your pet, that money is at risk. The money can be lost to their creditors, become part of a divorce settlement, or go to their heirs if they die. The money you set aside in a trust for the benefit of your pet is safe and can only be used for your pet's care.

You can name one person as the manager of trust assets and a different person as the pet caregiver. The manager of the trust assets can hold the pet caregiver accountable. You can control what happens to any money still in the trust when your pet dies.

Choosing pet caregivers (including alternates) who are willing to make the commitment is the most difficult part. Setting some money aside for your pet's care will go a long way in helping the person who is willing to make the commitment.

There are two ways to establish a pet trust. The first way to establish a pet trust is in a revocable living trust. Your trust rules can state that if you have a pet when you die, a portion of your estate will be held in trust for your pet's benefit. You can leave a specific amount per pet or provide a formula based on your pet's life expectancy to determine the amount per pet. Your successor trustee named in the trust rules would manage the money held in trust for the pet. The trustee would keep records of assets managed for the pet's benefit, but would not be required to share that information with the court. The trust rules would also state who was to receive the pet and be the caretaker and now owner of the pet. The advantage of using a living trust is that assets would immediately be available for your pet's care.

The second way is using a will. Your will can state that if you have a pet when you die, a portion of your estate will be held in trust for your pet's benefit. You can leave a specific amount per pet or provide a formula based on your pet's life expectancy to determine the amount per pet. Your will would also name a trustee who would manage the money held in trust for the pet. The trustee would be bonded and would have to provide annual accountings to the court to show how the trustee was investing and spending the money set aside for your pet. Your will would also state the name of the prospective caregiver/new owner for a pet. There are two disadvantages to this solution. First, the assets would not be immediately available for the care of your pet because they would first have to proceed through the probate system. The second disadvantage is the some of the funds would be used to pay the annual fees for the trustee's bond (and this can't be waived) and for the annual accounting fee.

With a revocable living trust or a will establishing a pet trust, you would have complete confidence is the welfare of your pet if anything happened to you. You would know that your pet would be provided for instead of going to a shelter or even worse—being euthanized.

Chapter 13

Unmarried Partners: Ways to Set Your Own Course

I was stationed at Naval Air Station Keflavik Iceland for eighteen months. The navy was responsible for all of the base activities, including the runway. The air force was responsible for everything having to do with the air force jets. Agreements had to be formed to coordinate everything so the navy knew its responsibilities and the air force knew its responsibilities. For example, the navy was responsible for making sure that the snow was removed from the runways, even though it was the air force who used the runways. Because it was a unique situation, the navy and air force created their own unique coordination solutions. Unmarried partners need to be aware of their unique coordination issues and solutions.

Consequences While Living

There are two issues to discuss for unmarried partners: the first is healthcare decisions, and the second is asset management.

Let's tackle healthcare decisions first. Healthcare decisions can be an emergency. So states have passed statutes that control who can make healthcare decisions for someone if it is an emergency and the person can't make the decision for themselves. A person can't make decisions for themselves if they are unconscious or receiving pain medication that prevents them from making decisions. The Virginia statute lists spouse first, then next blood relative. So if your partner is unconscious and a medical decision needs to be made, it may be your partner's parents who are making the medical decision. The parents may defer to you, but they would have the legal responsibility to make the decision.

The second issue is asset management for any asset in your partner's name alone. See <u>Chapter 6</u> for a complete explanation about the conservator appointment process. However, even if you are granted permission to access an asset owned by your partner, you will only be able to spend it on them and not yourself. It doesn't matter to the law that your partner was supporting you.

<u>Consequences at Death</u>

It is a fact that when a person dies their assets are left behind. Sometimes people do not have a plan for their asset distribution. Sometimes people do not designate who they want to receive an asset. Asset distribution needs to be settled, so states have statutes as default rules to achieve asset distribution by default. The Virginia statute states spouse first and then next blood relative. I have a client who received an unexpected check in the mail from the estate of a distant cousin she had heard of but didn't know. She received that check under the default rules for distribution.

Now let's apply the state statute to unmarried partners. If Tim owns the house that he and Marilyn live in, what happens to the house when Tim dies? Because the house is in his name alone with no beneficiary, the statute decides who is now the owner of the house. One thing is sure—it isn't Marilyn. The new owner could be Tim's children, or Tim's parents, or even Tim's siblings.

State statute also applies to who controls your remains when you are deceased. Spouse is first with next blood relatives next. Someone else would be deciding funeral arrangements and burial or cremation. Worst case is that you could be excluded from your partner's funeral.

There are Solutions

There is a solution to all of these issues, and that is to have an estate plan. Remember that the state statutes are the default rules. With estate planning documents, you can name anyone you want. You can choose who will make your healthcare decisions with a Healthcare Power of Attorney. You can choose who will manage your assets with a General Power of Attorney. You can choose what will happen to your assets with a living trust or a will. You can choose who will make the decisions regarding your remains when you are gone with your will or a Disposition of Remains document.

Declassified Secret #5

There are specific steps you need to know to prepare to get underway.

Chapter 14: PMS the Navy Way: Planned Maintenance Schedule for Your Estate Plan

Chapter 14 explains why estate planning is not a one and done event. A must read if your estate planning documents are more than three years old.

Chapter 15: How to Take the Next Step in Getting Your Own Unsinkable Battlegroup Estate Plan

Chapter 15 provides a step-by-step action plan for you. What you need to do next. A must read for everyone. There is an offer in this chapter that you are going to want to grab.

CHAPTER 14

PMS The Navy Way: Planned Maintenance Schedule for Your Estate Plan

For everything mechanical, the navy has a maintenance schedule. The object is to monitor and perform preventive maintenance to avoid mechanical breakdowns at sea. It's just like regularly changing the oil in your car and flushing the radiator at scheduled mileage intervals. Your estate plan should also have a maintenance schedule, because a malfunction or breakdown can be costly emotionally and financially for you and your family.

Change is going to happen no matter how hard we try to stand still. If nothing else, we are a day older than we were yesterday. It is futile to resist change. As you've heard it said, "Only diamonds are forever." Estate planning documents are not forever. We wish that signing our estate planning documents was a one-time thing, because we feel great relief and peace of mind after signing.

Lots of changes can drive revisions to your documents:

1. You get married.

2. You get divorced.

3. You have children.

4. Your children have children.

5. You get or get rid of assets such as real estate or stock.

6. You are single but have a significant other.

7. You have or your children have stepchildren or adopted children, and you want them to be included as heirs.

8. The law changes.

9. You get a pet and want to provide for them.

10. You buy an asset and forget to put the title in your trust's name.

11. Someone you selected as an agent under a power of attorney or as executor dies.

Many times these changes go unrecognized, which is why regular reviews are very important. I was the speaker at a Red Hat group luncheon. One of the members was proudly showing photos of her new grandchild. During lunch, she told me that she already had an estate plan. I asked her two questions:

(1) Would she want her daughter's inheritance to go to her new child if her daughter died?

(2) Does her will have a provision to hold onto the child's inheritance for management until the child is older than eighteen?

She said yes to the first question. She said I don't know to the second question. She did not recognize that a change had occurred that might drive a change to her estate plan.

Parents also need to update their estate plan when they have children. Movie star Keith Ledger's will left everything to his parents. He didn't update his will when his daughter was born. His parents turned his estate over to his daughter, but they didn't have to. If they made a simple disclaimer to his estate (declining the inheritance), his child will receive all that money when she has her eighteenth birthday. By the way, the mother of his child didn't get anything.

Sometimes we think that we have plenty of time to get things done, like the transfer of asset title to a living trust. I prepared a living trust for Karen. Karen's situation was unusual. You hear about children being kidnapped by a parent and wonder if it really happens. It happened to Karen. Her ex-husband took their two young children to a foreign country, and Karen was unable to see them again. When her children became adults, they did not want a relationship with their mother. We met for a review of her estate plan. Karen was leaving everything to her three best friends. We talked about her 401k because she admitted that she still had her deceased mother as her beneficiary on her 401k. I said that she needed to fix that by changing the beneficiary on her 401k to her trust so it would go to her friends. Karen didn't get around to it before she died. Karen died unexpectedly. The financial institution has their own rules about who gets the 401k when the named beneficiary is deceased. Their rules state that it goes to Karen's children, which is *not* what she wanted. It was too late to fix this problem.

I recommend a review of your estate plan every three years. When steering a ship, all it takes is a small error to get you completely off course and miss your destination. Having assets incorrectly titled, wrong beneficiaries names, no beneficiary named, and more can cause your estate plan to fail. If your estate plan fails, your loved ones are going to have not only a headache but also heartache.

CHAPTER 15

How to Take the Next Step in Getting Your Own Unsinkable Battlegroup Estate Plan

You don't have to figure everything out and have all the answers before you can make an appointment.

IF:

- you want to know what you <u>don't know</u> about estate planning,

- you have been resisting or procrastinating because you don't know what to do and are afraid to ask,

- you want a better understanding of the estate plan you already have and want to see if your attorney missed an important issue,

THEN: You want to make an appointment for your complimentary Estate Planning Discovery Consultation. You will receive ninety minutes of legal advice specific to you. All of your questions will be answered. More importantly, you will find out about hidden estate planning issues that can cost your family thousands of dollars and create a crisis situation for them. There is never any pressure or obligation.

You Can Be On Your Way to Protecting Your Family, Avoiding a Crisis, and Making It Easier On Your Family When You Are Gone

Our Approach to Estate Planning is Different

A career in the navy brought me to Hampton Roads. At the sixteen-year mark, I was thinking about what I wanted to do at the end of my twenty-year navy career. I discovered that Regent University was starting evening law school classes. Attending night classes extended the time to graduation to four years. Perfect! I had four years left in the navy to complete my twenty. So that is what I did—I wore a navy officer's uniform by day and attended law school classes at night. While in law school, I chose estate planning as my legal area of expertise. I learned how to be a traditional estate planning attorney by working at a law firm on the peninsula for two years. When I opened my own law firm ten years ago, I decided to redefine the estate planning experience.

My firm does not charge by the hour but by the service at a flat rate, so there are NO surprises with regard to fees. We speak in plain English and never use legalese. We ask leading questions, really listen, and offer customized solutions. We have also studied long-term care planning, which qualifies the firm to target the special requirements of senior clients.

Relax. Ask Questions. Smile.

We treat everyone as our honored guest because that is what you are. We are friendly and smile a lot. You don't need to worry that we will be snooty and condescending like some attorneys. We are down to earth and will answer your concerns and questions honestly and completely.

We use plain English and will explain any legal terms you need to know. We draw diagrams and makes notes for you to take with you. This meeting is not scary (we have a candy dish) or intimidating.

At the end of your meeting with us, you will know our recommendations and exactly what your investment for our services will be.

No surprises, no obligation, and no pressure.

<u>That is what we promise.</u>

Special Offer from
Linda M. Sherfey, P.C.
The Estate Planning Solution

We don't want any barrier to stand in the way of you finding out about the 5 Declassified Estate Planning Secrets You Can't Afford to Ignore.

This book is designed to inform you before you meet with us.

After we meet, this book will be a reference to remind you of our discussion.

But wait, there's more!

You can meet with us for ninety minutes for a FREE estate planning consultation. This book is a general guide. During our meeting, we dive deep into your unique situation. You know your family, situation, and goals. We know the law. Together, we create a customized plan for you.

But wait, there's more!

If you bring this book with you to your FREE estate planning consultation, you will receive a $100 discount when choosing a complete estate plan.

You have this guidebook, now you need your customized plan.

The waiting time to meet with us is two to four weeks. So call now, because you'll have plenty of time to finish reading this book before we meet.

Call 757-966-9700 right now to get started.

Appendix A

Ten Questions You Must Ask Before Choosing an Estate Planning Attorney

You wouldn't ask your plumber to do your wiring, so don't ask a real estate attorney to do your will. It is not their area of expertise. These are the ten questions you should ask before hiring an estate planning attorney to help you plan for the well-being of yourself, your family, your life, and your money. Our answers are in bold.

1. What percentage of your practice is estate planning?

Our answer is 100 percent.

2. Are all of your fees flat fees without any surprises?

Yes, agreed to in advance.

3. What happens when I call with questions about my documents two years after my documents are completed?

We never charge for answering questions about the documents we prepared for you.

4. What if my family needs help when I am mentally incapacitated or gone?

We provide thirty minutes at no charge to answer a family member's questions and provide guidance on using your estate planning documents, on the telephone, so they don't have to wait for an appointment.

5. Do you know about long-term care planning so my family will have the powers they need in my estate planning documents to qualify me for government benefits if I can't do it for myself?

Yes. We call them senior super powers, and there are three powers that need to be in every senior's General Power of Attorney.

6. Do you draft your own estate planning documents, or do you use a document system that is used by thousands of attorneys across the United States?

We use Wealth Counsel as our document drafting system. The monthly license fee is expensive, but we want the very best for our clients. We want the expertise of attorneys all across the United States so our documents are kept up to date with the latest developments in the law.

7. Can you help me make the hard decisions of what to do with my assets and who to choose to act my behalf?

Yes, so don't let decision-making difficulties hold you back. We have seen lots of different family situations, and together, we can create a customized solution that is just right for you.

8. If I choose a living trust, do you help me make sure my assets are titled in the right way?

Yes. We create your unique spreadsheet list of assets with clear directions on what to do with that asset: change title or make the trust the beneficiary of an asset. The spreadsheet becomes your action checklist.

9. Will you stay in touch with me? How often do you communicate with me? Will my family be able to find you if they need you?

We publish a monthly print newsletter. Your family will be able to find us by getting your mail and finding our newsletter. Every newsletter issue has contact information and much more.

10. What happens when things change in my life? Does my planning fee include a periodic review of my plan? What if I want to make changes to my plan?

Periodic reviews of your plan are essential. Included in your plan are reviews every three years. We can meet for an hour with no additional fee to review your situation and see if anything needs to be changed in your documents. There is a fee for revisions.

You won't find another estate planning attorney in Hampton Roads that has all of these answers. Call 757-966-9700 today to schedule your complimentary estate planning appointment with us. Plan on at least ninety minutes of legal estate planning information about what is possible for you.

APPENDIX B

How My Naval Career Provides Excellent Attorney Skills

I served the better part of my adult life as an officer in the United States Navy. I learned some very valuable skills due to the nature of being in the military and as a result of the variety of jobs I performed. I was an unrestricted line officer. What that means is that I didn't have a specialty. My specialty was learning new jobs skills quickly, because almost every time I transferred to a new assignment, I had a completely different job.

Oceanographic Watch Officer: Naval Oceanographic Processing Facility, Pearl Harbor, Hawaii and Coos Bay, Oregon
Looking Below the Surface

Undersea surveillance at Ford Island in the middle of Pearl Harbor, Hawaii and next at Coos Bay, Oregon were my first two assignments in the navy. It was during the Cold War, and the navy wanted to know where the Soviet submarines were hiding. At the time, the command's mission of hunting and locating Soviet submarines was classified Top Secret. I couldn't tell anyone what I did when I went to work. The navy invested months and money in my training, so two tours of duty for the same mission were required. As a watch officer, I was responsible for a division of eight to ten elite enlisted personnel in my watch section. Looking for Soviet submarines was a 365 day, 24/7 mission. I became proficient at looking below the surface for hidden problems.

It is called collateral duty when you are also assigned a part-time job. On my way to Coos Bay, Oregon I attended navy legal officer training at Newport, Rhode Island for thirty days. The day I reported for duty at Coos Bay, I was assigned a JAGMAN investigation for a murder and suicide that occurred at the command shortly before I arrived. My investigative report was so complete, nobody had any questions all the way up to the admiral. The navy lawyers said they had never seen a report make it all the way to the top without questions before.

Assistant Public Affairs Officer: Navy Submarine Base Bangor, Silverdale, Washington Coordinating Complex Events & Public Speaking

My next tour of duty was public relations at what was then the only Trident submarine base in the navy, at Silverdale, Washington. Trident submarines are the Rolls-Royce of the submarine force. The base hosted a lot of high-level visits from congressmen, NATO Nuclear Planning Group, admirals, and even astronauts. My assignment was to coordinate their tours of the navy base, submarines, and other commands. Since I was crafting detailed time lines for submarine tours, I had access to the Top Secret messages containing the submarine schedules. I became very proficient at public speaking and creating presentations. I also was responsible for the base newspaper.

Student: Navy Postgraduate School, Monterrey, California Looking at Problems from Different Perspectives for Solutions

Then I attended the Navy Postgraduate School at Monterrey, California as a student. I obtained a masters degree in joint command, control, and communications (also known as systems technology in the civilian world). This was my first experience of a set of rooms with special access requirements because they were full of classified information. At Washington, DC, we toured the agencies responsible for the president's communications when he is out of town. We also toured the "hidden in a mountain" complex designed for the possibility of nuclear war. I became proficient at looking at problems from different perspectives for solutions.

Administration Officer: Fleet Anti-Submarine Warfare Training Center
Protecting Sensitive Information & Record Keeping

I transferred across the United States to Norfolk, Virginia. I was the administration officer at the Fleet Anti-Submarine Warfare Training Center. This was the first training command I attended when I became an officer on my way to Hawaii. I felt like I had come home. I was the commanding officer and executive officer's right hand person in everything administrative. I was also the command security officer. Any information about submarines is going to be classified at least secret. As you can imagine, at a training command about submarines, there were a lot of training manuals, presentations, and even exams containing secret information. I became proficient at protecting sensitive information and record keeping.

Family Service Center Director: Naval Air Station Keflavik, Iceland
Getting Along with Everyone

My tour in Norfolk was cut short when the navy downsized by closing some commands, including the Fleet Anti-Submarine Warfare Training Center. So off I went to Naval Air Station, Keflavik, Iceland for eighteen months as the Family Service Center director. Staff at the Family Service Center included one navy chief, three civil service social workers, and two Icelanders. The center supported both navy and air force personnel. I became proficient at working with and getting along with all types of people.

Assistant Port Operations Officer, Naval Station Norfolk, Virginia
Managing Paperwork & Deadlines

Then back to the United States as the assistant port operations officer at Naval Station Norfolk, Virginia. Naval Station Norfolk is the largest navy base in the world. At that time, the department was responsible for eight tugboats, their crews, and other personnel who were responsible for getting the navy ships and submarines in and out of port safely and on time. The department had 150 personnel, and I was responsible for all administrative matters. I became proficient in managing lots of paperwork and deadlines.

Toward the end of this tour, the commanding officer reassigned me as the public relations officer for the base. I was responsible for the tour office (daily buses provide civilians a tour of the base), any interactions with the press, and the base newspaper. A big project the commanding officer assigned to me was his change of command. As you can imagine, the change of command ceremony at the world's largest navy base was a big deal. This particular commanding officer was very demanding and vocal when he was unhappy. There had better be no typos in his change of command program, and nothing could go wrong. I kept track of everything I coordinated and created a how-to binder for the next person so they wouldn't have to start with nothing, like I did. I do mean everything—including where to buy the colored tassels for the programs. I became proficient at organizing a large project, proofreading, and dealing with difficult people.

Law School Student: Regent University, Virginia Beach, Virginia
Juggling a Full-Time Job and Full-Time Schoolwork

I am a planner by nature, so at the sixteen-year point, I was thinking about what I wanted to do next with my life. I found out by accident (or was it fate) that Regent University Law School was starting an evening law school program in 1998. I found out about the night program in January, had to have my application in by March, took the law school entrance exam (LSAT) in June, was accepted by the school in July, and started law school in August. Whew! When you attend law school at night, it takes four years to graduate. I was a navy officer in uniform by day and law school student in jeans at night. Fortunately for me, I have the best husband ever, and he is always very supportive when I want to tackle something new.

Administration Officer: Navy & Marine Corps Intelligence Training Center, Virginia Beach, Virginia
Knowing and Applying the Rules

Fortunately, I was able to stay in the Norfolk area for my next assignment, so I could stay in law school. It almost didn't happen. My heart sank as I listened to a voice message from my detailer (the person who writes transfer orders) saying I might have to report to a command in Japan instead of my current orders to the Navy and Marine Corps Intelligence Training Command. She said I was one of three people being considered for the assignment in Japan.

Fortunately, I was not sidetracked to Japan, and instead kept the orders I already had and transferred to the Navy and Marine Corps Intelligence Training Command at Virginia Beach, Virginia. I was the commanding officer and executive officer's right hand person, as the administration officer. The command trained navy and marine corps enlisted personnel and officers as intelligence specialists. Most of the enlisted assigned to the command as students were fresh out of boot camp eighteen-year-olds. Sometimes I would also assist as the legal officer, and there was a lot to do. Students would get themselves into trouble by going on the wrong parts of the beach that were restricted, staying out too late, missing class—you get the picture. I also was the person the command relied on for knowing the ins and outs of managing civil service personnel. I became proficient at knowing and applying the rules.

Programming Officer: Commander-in-Chief Atlantic Fleet, Norfolk, Virginia Budgeting—Really?

My last navy assignment was at Commander-in-Chief Atlantic Fleet in the Fleet Training Directorate. The admiral is responsible for all the ships and sailors in the Atlantic. I learned about the navy budgeting process.

As a collateral duty, I also served as the senior officer on administrative discharge boards. Navy personnel don't have to go to a court-martial trial to be discharged for less serious offenses. A board of three officers has the authority to recommend an administrative discharge. A JAG (Judge Advocate General) officer (real attorney) defends the accused. Evidence is presented and witnesses are questioned, just like a trial, but there are far fewer restrictions on what can be presented to the board.

I had another collateral duty as a brig magistrate. Commanding officers have the authority to send their personnel to the brig (jail). However, within a limited time, a brig magistrate reviews the evidence and makes a decision as to whether the sailor will stay in the brig or be released to the command. I also served on court-martial juries. So even though I was not a JAG attorney, I had a thorough knowledge of and experience in the military justice system.